The Fight for Belle Vue

&

The Field of Power

Two Plays
by
Travis Weekes

These plays by Travis Weekes in its printed form are fully protected under copyright laws and are subject to royalty. All rights, including professional, amateur, motion picture, recitation, lecturing, public reading, radio and television broadcast, and the rights of translation into foreign languages, are strictly reserved. No public or private performance or reading—professional or amateur—may be given without the permission of the author. All inquiries should be addressed to the publisher at info@caribbeanreads.com.

About the playwright:
Dr. Travis Weekes is a Saint Lucian poet and dramatist and currently a lecturer in Theatre at the Department of Creative and Festival Arts UWI, Saint Augustine.
Other plays by Dr. Weekes are "Stepping Out", "Doing it for Kenna," "In Memoriam," and "The Snake Exterminator."

Many thanks to the Campus Research and Publication Fund Committee, UWI, Saint Augustine, for funding this project.

The Fight for Belle Vue Text copyright © 2010 Travis Weekes
The Field of Power Text copyright © 2015 Travis Weekes
Front cover photo copyright 2017 Pascal Maillet-Contoz. Used with permission.

CaribbeanReads Publishing, Washington DC, 20006
First Edition
All rights reserved.
Printed in the USA
ISBN: 978-1-7338299-7-7 (paperback)

TABLE OF CONTENTS

FOREWORD i

THE FIGHT FOR BELLE VUE 1
    PRODUCTIONS 2
    CAST OF CHARACTERS 4
    SETTING 4
    PROLOGUE 5
    ACT ONE 10
    ACT TWO 64

THE FIELD OF POWER 91
    PRODUCTIONS 92
    CAST IN ORDER OF APPEARANCE 92
    CHARACTERS 93
    SETTING 93
    TIME 93
    PROLOGUE 94
    ACT ONE 97

GLOSSARY 132

FOREWORD

When I wrote these plays I wanted to inspire young actors to participate in a project that would require them to utilize cultural material from our Creole Culture. I wanted performers to recognize the elements of theatre in the Creole forms around them and the immense potential of using those forms to speak to the social and political challenges facing our environment. Thus I went to ritual, the Creole ritual of the folk. I also went to the myth and folklore that we absorbed as children during the oral tradition of storytelling.

I am a part of a tradition of course, and the best examples of playwrights before me who delved into the folk culture to create theatre were the twin brothers Derek and Roderick Walcott of Saint Lucia and Errol Hill of Trinidad and Tobago. The close relationship that developed between Hill and the twin brothers during the 1950's, which coincided with the decline of the British Empire in the Caribbean, stemmed from a mutual interest in the process of shaping a unique West Indian theatre.

Pioneers

The theatre envisaged by those pioneers sought to create a novel aesthetic. To this end, the Walcott twins experimented with every major cultural folk form in Saint Lucia. The Flower Societies: La Rose and La Maguerite were Roderick's main resource. Three of his plays, "The Banjo Man," "Chanson Marianne," and "Romeo èk Violet" utilize the music, dance, colour inherent in the pageantry of the festivals. Yet he also explored storytelling and magic in "Malfinis," the Papa Diable in "The Devil at Christmas," the Steel Band in "Strove Tuesday March," and the Kèlè in "Cassian and Capricorn."

Derek, the elder of the twin brothers utilized the wake rituals for "The Sea at Dauphin" and "Malcochon;" the street theatre of the Papa Diable for "Ti Jean and His Brothers;" the La Diablesse for "Dream On Monkey Mountain;" the Flower Festivals and Carnival for "The Haitian Earth;" and the Steel Pan for "Steel;" among others.

Errol Hill was part of the initiative, exploring the Steel Band in "The Ping Pong;" the wake ritual in "Dance Bongo;" and stick-fighting and Obeah in "Man Better Man." A Trinidadian, Hill eventually settled on the Trinidad Carnival as the repository of the crucial elements for the making of a national theatre and published a treatise on the subject entitled, "The Trinidad Carnival: Mandate for a National Theatre."

Among the three playwrights, Derek's drama suggests the most scrupulous incorporation of selected elements of those rituals crafted within a more neatly developed dramatic structure fused from Creole and Western narrative forms. In what is perhaps his most popular play, "Ti Jean and His Brothers," the traditional storyteller meets the device of Greek chorus in the creation of three animal characters: Bird, Frog, and Cricket. In this play, the animal characters are also significant to the characterization of Papa Bois and the three brothers. They begin the play with a slightly modified version of the traditional 'Queek Quack" and then proceed to introduce the principal characters and setting. As the plot unfolds, the playwright has written in songs and movement within and in between scenes. This allows spaces for music and dance.

Storytelling

The traditional storytelling form offers a ready dramatic structure. The Storyteller/Kontè appears at the beginning, somewhere in the middle, and at the end of the production when the conflict is resolved. At this point it becomes more apparent that the storyteller is the voice of playwright who clarifies the moral of the final outcome and closes the event.

In Derek Walcott's "Malcochon," a similar structure is adopted. The Conteur begins the story, introduces the principal characters, and interjects a couple of times during the action to describe the setting, create the mood, or move the plot along. These interjections also create spaces for music and dance. He then reappears after the resolution of the conflict to close the play and articulate to the audience, the moral vision of the author.

Another Caribbean playwright who used the storytelling tradition to structure his drama was Jamaican playwright, Trevor Rhone. His play "Old Story Time" is a prime example. Here, Pa Ben, the storyteller, is also a major character in the play, crucial to the plot and to the shaping of other characters. However, like the traditional storyteller, Pa Ben also possesses the knowledge of the folksongs and dances that he can use to stimulate members of his audience to join in and assist him in delivering the narrative. Rhone has actually written an audience into the script from which he derives the actors for his performance.

Theatre is inseparable from the desire of human beings to tell stories, to recount, to relate the experiences of the family, of the tribe. In oral cultures, the storyteller was indeed the historian who passed on knowledge from one generation to the next. The storyteller had a ready audience who gathered in designated places to experience the unfolding of his narrative. In this context the act of storytelling was a performance and invariably the storyteller facilitated other participants: musicians, singers, actors, and dancers, to assist in the delivery of the stories. Herein lay the very close relationship between storytelling and theatre.

Thus, storytelling has played a significant role in the cultural life of traditional Caribbean society. Perhaps this is because the majority of Caribbean people originated from West Africa, the home of the Griots. In the Francophone Caribbean (former colonies of the French), storytelling is referred to as "Conte" (French) written in creole as 'Kont", meaning "to tell", or "to relate". Thus the storyteller is referred to as the Conteur, (French), or Kontè (Creole).

The Kont

The Kont tradition is associated with Wake ceremonies, which are held on evenings in the family compound when someone has died. In Wake ceremonies, the Storyteller is the central character. He is the memory of the community. The stories, which he relates to entertain his audience are also a tribute to the deceased and to the community that he leaves behind. His repertoire of narratives: stories, riddles, jokes, and songs are familiar to the audience because each generation produces storytellers who learn to recount significant events in the life of the community.

However, in as much as stories are based on actual events, each story is a work of art and the best storytellers are very fine artists. While many storytellers retell stories that have come through generations, the best storytellers are those who make adjustments to the narratives, often making them more relevant to happenings within their community. These are the ones who possess the voice, and the practice of skilfully using that voice, to keep the ear of their audiences and invoke their responses. They could sing; the right line or two would cue in the audience and bring out a chorus of responses from them.

Storytelling and Playwriting

In keeping with the tradition, some Caribbean playwrights have demonstrated their skill as master literary storytellers. When these playwrights import the character of the storyteller unto the stage, not only are they attempting to recreate the yard setting of the traditional storyteller, but they are aiming as well to transfer the dramatic structure and elements of theatre inherent in the form. The storyteller is the activist who "jump starts" the audience and propels them into the drama. He also introduces the plot and characters, bridges the acts or scenes and closes the show.

The character of the Storyteller written into a play, upon his very entrance unto the stage, and immediate "call" out to the audience, triggers its memory and imagination and transports it to that space where stories of the community are shared. The memory stirred is of the outdoor setting in the yard, neatly swept, under a tree. It is a place of warmth and laughter, of sharing and camaraderie. It is an intergenerational space where some sit on a bench, or on the ground, where children lean upon their mothers, aunts or grandmothers and listen intently, eyes fastened upon the Storyteller. The story is filled with characters, animals, and humans; a plot is developed, conflicts resolved and a moral lesson driven home.

In the plays published here, I use the traditional storytelling form to provide a narrative structure for the theatre, but the drama derives its energy from clashing religious values, individual ambitions, and political trajectories. In "The Fight for Belle Vue", the Kèlè, an African-derived ritual, generates the ontological angst of the main characters. Here, my choice of the Kèlè as an embodiment of the social conscience of the community of Belle Vue, is as much an attempt to rid us of the prejudices created by colonial discourse against our own, as it is a strategy to draw out the theatre of the folk. The ritual, now extinct, was practised in the North Eastern region of Saint Lucia and involved the sacrifice of a sheep to the African deities of Shango and Ogun. It was an elaborate ritual, a full theatrical performance with elements of magic, music, poetry, dance, and costume, which unfortunately is no longer practiced as it came under severe pressure from the Christian authorities and the 'civilizing" mission of the state.

Religion

The demonization of the religious and cultural expressions of the descendants of Africans by the Catholic Church is hypocritical as this church has observed the most horrendous, bloody atrocities committed by Christian colonizers against their subjects during the period of colonization. The legacy of this demonization is evident in the self-degradation of too many of the people who reside in the communities that once practised the Kèlè. Not only do many of those people seem ashamed of their past but they also demonstrate a lack of understanding and appreciation for the role that their culture can play in safeguarding their social and physical environment.

The attitude of church and state to the religious rites of the descendants of Africans also extended to the dances associated with those rites even after those religious practices became extinct. Therefore, whereas the state has endorsed and supported the European derived ballroom dance of the Quadrille popular in the spaces within its purview, those other dances among the rural folk associated more directly with the Afro-derived rituals received comparatively little state support. The result is that those dances have either become extinct in the communities or are fledgling and underdeveloped.

Music and Dance

For this reason, in the two plays of this collection, I draw from the music and dance elements of the oral tradition of storytelling to begin the drama. The director has tremendous leeway here in terms of choice as he can explore the various dances from the wake traditions in the Caribbean to grab the audience's attention before the Storyteller actually commences his story.

The familiarity of song and dance narratives, invoke the memories of the audience, bringing them closer to the performance. Not only does this keep the audience's attention but the interaction affords them the opportunity to participate in the event, to feel part of the community and give real support to the activity

One of my reasons therefore for writing Afro-Caribbean dances in the plays is to challenge performers to learn them, and to be led by choreographers interested in expanding the range of possibilities offered by work-shopping those dances. The vocabulary was Bèlè Kont but the technique was Jazz. The aesthetic was the elegance, finesse even, of the folk. The other reason for the choice of folk dances was to help perpetuate the intricate rhythms and tones of the drum required for the folk dances. I wanted more young male performing artists to develop an interest in drumming.

Thus during the rehearsal process, I brought together musicians, singers, drummers, and choreographers who possessed an intimate knowledge of the dance narratives, to interact with my performers. Richard Ambrose, a dancer and choreographer who was formally trained in the French (Creole) island of Guadeloupe, worked closely with Leo Amedee, another dancer and choreographer who acquired his skills from the family and community of the Saint Lucian creole community of Fond Assau.

Although the Bèlè traditions are quickly dying in Saint Lucia, some of the cultural elements such as the drumming, the dances, and the songs, are still embedded in the memory of the folk. The choice therefore to create a character like Sandra in "The Fight for Bell Vue," a lead dancer who is intent on safeguarding the Kèlè, forces a director to seek choreographers and performers who are interested in dances associated with Afro-rituals of the Caribbean. Similarly, in "The Field of Power" when Madame Sajès urges Eva to use the Bèlè as a cultural weapon as she struggles for her soul in the fight against the Ladjablès, actor and choreographer are being forced to make creative and dramatic use of the dance form.

Caribbean folk music is of tremendous significance to the plays. The folk songs used in the plays are taken from Saint Lucia, but directors are welcome to use songs from their own territories. Indeed, the transfer of music from the oral tradition to the stage utilizes the call and response structure typical of Caribbean folk songs that invites audience interaction. In fact, the music of the plays comes from the ordinary percussive instruments used traditionally by the Caribbean folk. The songs used in the plays form part of a genre that has a common rhythm and melodic structure throughout many islands of the Caribbean. The drum is common of course because it is central. However, where necessary, the Chak-Chak (maracas) and Ti-bwa can be added. A cuatro also adds a great sound. Of course, directors are free to employ electronic instruments. Although not entirely necessary, the sensuous impact of strings and keyboards on the audience also sets the mood for the respective scenes.

There is a huge reservoir of dances from the rural yard in the Caribbean that a director can draw from for staging the plays. Dances are of dramatic significance to these plays in several ways. They are written into very particular junctures so as to break the monotony of the dialogue. The colour of the costumes and movement of the performers hold tremendous visual appeal. Since they are dances of the folk that the general audience can recognize and identify with, they enhance the popular appeal of the production. Thus for the reasons mentioned above directors are advised to work closely with a choreographer who is willing to explore/workshop the dances from the various African derived rituals of the Caribbean and guide the actors and dancers creatively.

The dances employed in the play derive from the wake ceremonies and fertility rituals practised by the descendants of Africans in Caribbean society. In Saint Lucia, the Kont, Kutumba and Kèlè rituals provide a wealthy resource for theatre practitioners. While those rituals are no longer practised, the dances which were integral to their performance survive in various forms and styles. The dances which were performed in the inaugural performances of the play here are similar to those from the Dinki Mini and Kumina traditions of Jamaica as well as the Bongo tradition of Trinidad and Tobago. In the territories formerly colonized by the French such as Martinque, Guadeloupe, Dominica, and Saint Lucia many folk dances of the yard are referred to as Bèlè, French (Belaire). The Bèlè has also been a popular dance in Trinidad and Tobago where French planters migrated with their enslaved Africans in the 18th century. The Bèlè dances bear very close similarities to the other dances of the rural yard in other Caribbean territories.

Set and Backdrop

These plays should not make any strenuous technical demands upon the director. Here dance and drama set against simple backdrops are quite helpful in locating the action of the plays. "The Fight for Belle Vue" is located on a Banana estate above which we would see, on the one end, the house of Tonne and on the other, the house of Kosh. Below the house of Tonne should be the Mango Tree where Sandra practises her dances and meets with Garvin. The set here would simply be a long bench upon which Sandra would sit with Tonne or with Garvin, when necessary.

A backdrop can also locate the action of the "The Field of Power." The action takes place in the village of Derrière Morne, above which is the mountain, the home of the La Diablesse (Ladjablès). Therefore, a backdrop should foreground the poor village with the mountain above in the background. A light beyond the mountain could suffice as a symbol of the Land of Opportunity. The stage would be divided into two; the space of Madame Sajès and the space of the Ladjablès. One bench is needed before the space of Madame Sajès to accommodate Eva when she is grating the cassava. A chair or stool is required before the space of the

La Diablesse where Eva would sit for the transformation scene.

Conclusion

The production of this text is the result of decades of studying the craft of leading Caribbean dramatists, in particular Derek and Roderick Walcott, Errol Hill, Denis Scott and Trevor Rhone. The methodology is derived from a praxis of studying how to root the Elements of Drama in the indigenous culture of the Caribbean. Therefore, the composition of the plays followed a process of study, writing and rewriting, rehearsal and staging. It is my hope that "The Field of Power" and "The Fight for Belle Vue" can provide additional material for the dramatists interested in exploring theatrical potential of Caribbean cultural forms. The plays have been very successfully staged with older teenagers and therefore can also be useful for theatre students at both the secondary and tertiary levels.

The plays are also useful for stimulating discussions regarding tradition versus modernity, politics and society, youth and ambition, Man and his environment. For this reason, they may also be useful for teachers and students of Caribbean Literature and Social Studies. The author is very pleased to share. Welcome once again to the joy of Caribbean Theatre.

Give thanks.

Travis Weekes PhD
UWI, Saint Augustine

For Allan Weekes,
my father and mentor

The Fight for Belle Vue

PRODUCTIONS

"The Fight For Belle Vue" was first staged at the University of the West Indies, Cave Hill, Barbados, on November 6, 2010 with the following cast and crew:

CAST IN ORDER OF APPEARANCE

Kontè	Danielle Edwards
Kosh	Celsus Henry
Tonne	Kervon Lewis
Sandra	Giselle Volney
Garvin	David Francis
Meredith	Ndala Mills
Natasha	Jerelle Joseph
Henri	Imbert Daniel

DANCERS

Vicky Bailey	Liz Joseph
Kiera DeFreitas	Naomi Jude
Mathelda Demar	Shemanna McLawrence
Khadya Florius	Blossom Paul
Tricia Herman	Kyra Paul
Cindy Jn. Baptiste	Kittel Raphael

STAGE HANDS AND EXTRAS

Larry Aguiste	Casey Destang
Kareem Alleyne	Vilan Edward
Kerron Bruney	Adrian Paris

TECHNICAL TEAM

Playwright: Travis Weekes
Director : Khrystal Lucien
Choreographer : Melanie Paul-Wilson
Costume Manager : Alberta William
Backdrop : Cozier Frederick

The play was later staged by the author on May 25, 2017 at the National Cultural Centre, Saint Lucia with the following cast and crew:

CAST IN ORDER OF APPEARANCE

Kontè	Regica Hippolyte
Kosh	Junior Placide
Tonne	Alex Elibox
Sandra	Tish Demar
Garvin	Rohan Arthur
Meredith	Ashnell Aimable
Natasha	Edel William
Henri	Yakub Nestor

DANCERS

Jeannel Alexander	Desire Jn. Baptiste
Alex Desir	James Jones
Kyle Dolort	Ashley Leon
Bianca Edwin	Shanaii Mesmain
Mercedes Fanis	Elam Norville
Sami Felix	Seanelle Pierre
Tene Florentville	Kassi Pierre –Louis
Merrick Hippolyte	Fidele Simeon
Lauri Hutchinson Jr.	Jasmine Suffren

TECHNICAL TEAM

Director and Playwright: Travis Weekes
Assistant Stage Manager: (Lighting) Cassie St Ange
Assistant Stage Manager: (props) Colletta Gilbert
Stage Manager: Khrystal Lucien
Choreographer: Richard Ambrose and Leo Amedee
Drummers: Leo Amedee and Charles Desrivieres
Set and Backdrop: Pablo Lucien

CAST OF CHARACTERS

(In order of appearance)

Kontè:	Storyteller: Male or female, elderly.
Kosh:	Tonne's brother, farmer and construction worker, mid sixties
Tonne:	a farmer, widower, late sixties.
Sandra:	his daughter. A dancer and university student, twenty-two
Garvin:	A teacher and political aspirant. In love with Sandra. Early thirties.
Meredith:	Kosh's wife. Farmer and housewife. Late fifties.
Natasha:	daughter of Kosh and Meredith, an actress, twenty

Henri Laroche: An investor, white mid-thirties.

Drummers, dancers, singers.

SETTING

The present:

In the heights of a rural community in the Caribbean. Backdrop: A banana plantation interspersed with a few tall trees.

Stage left:

A banana shed stacked with banana boxes, some banana leaves and hands of green bananas lying loosely.

Stage right:

A long bench.

PROLOGUE

(As the lights come up, drummers, singers and dancers perform a very rhythmic folk song then Kontè begins the story. Kontè is at stage right while dancers are at stage left.)

KONTÈ

Well, one time dey had two families, well,
Two families divided into one; descendants of the Djiné.
Two brothers, the elder one they was calling Tonne
and the younger one, dey was calling Kosh.
Both of them lived on that estate down dere, a big estate,
the one stretching from Belle Vue all the way down to Grand Sable.
Tonne and Kosh was doing well, well, well; very well.
Was the days of green gold, the whole estate covered with bananas.
Tonne and Kosh had plenty of workers, ploughing and planting
and ploughing and planting.

(Dancers perform a mime of workers, men and women of both families, planting bananas, reaping bananas, carrying bananas, washing them, singing as they work)
During the week everybody working hard, hard, hard.
Was truly a beautiful sight to see, the way everybody
Worked together, the men did the planting, and women too.
The women carried the bananas on their heads to the banana shed
and the younger men helped them, and the women washed the bananas
and packed them in the boxes and counted them
and the money was coming in strong every week
and Tonne build a big house and Kosh build a bigger one
and every weekend, everybody in their glory.
Oh..o..ooh, was a beautiful sight to see.

(Vigourous Folk Music. A group of dancers move in a circle, feasting on barbecue chicken, while a chantwelle sings and they respond in chorus)

KONTÈ
Everything was going well until till one day...

(Outside the shed.)

KOSH
Bananas finish!

TONNE
What?

KOSH
It finish, finish, finish. I not wasting my time. Twenty cents a pound? What is that? Buy your own fertilizer? What is that? No spray plane, what is that? One time the earth getting dry like it siding with Chiquitta. Another time the wind so hard the bananas cyan stand up. What is that? I finish today, I telling you, Tonne. I leaving worse than when man turn his back on a woman.

TONNE
Bétise. You leave bananas, what you goin' do? What you goin' eat? What your children going eat?

KOSH
Which children. They all gone 'bout their business already. You forget? Is only Meredith and myself.

TONNE
Yes but they have to eat too. Bétise, I tell you.

KOSH
I am a fisherman. You forget? I was a fisherman long before I start planting bananas. I still have my kannòt down Grand Sable. You forget I used to brave these big mama waves and go all St. Vincent and catch fish. You forget is I feed Belle Vue people? Besides I have sense and connections.

TONNE

That is history, Kosh. You talking thirty, forty years ago. You touching sixty years now. You will go into that sea down there for it to pull you into its belly and then vomit you for the crabs. There is plenty evil around so you better watch out.

KOSH

You always talk about evil. That is what keeping you back.

TONNE

And you blind you cannot see it. That is why you put it right under your roof.

KOSH

What you talking about Tonne? That is ignorance. Don't think that I cannot pick your nonsense. My wife is a born-again Christian woman. I standing here hearing you insulting her.

TONNE

I didn't mention anybody name. But if that's the sense you pick.

KOSH

Who else you talking about? How many people I have under my roof? I shouda never listen to you. I had my job in Martinique. I leave it to come and help you in the bananas and look what happen.

TONNE

You never say that when the money was flowing. Look at the size of the house you build. You never say that at all.

KOSH

I spend a lot of my own money on the house. I work five years in doing construction in Martinique. Is I send money for Papa to build the retaining wall after the hurricane. If it wasn't for me all that whole side of the hill there woulda be gone. If I had put all the money into the house, I would not

KOSH (continued)

find myself in this situation now where the bank want to seize the roof over my head. Although you have five years more than me, you was always the coward. You was always the one scared to leave the land. You love the smell of the pigs just as you love the talk of evil.

TONNE

I never hung my hat where my hand cannot reach. I am a Djiné and so are you. Aside from the land, our faith, and our music, the animals was all that we had. That's how Ma and Pa bring us up. Cows mean meat and milk. Sheep is our sacrifice. Pigs bring mud but they can bring the same money you like so much.

KOSH

You mad.

TONNE

Is you mad. If you leave bananas, what you goin' do?

KOSH

I have connections I tell you and I have a plan. One that will bring plenty money to both you and me. More money than Mama and Papa and their Mama and Papa and all of our family together ever dream of.

TONNE

Where de money coming from? Dat sound like devil business!

KOSH

I cyan tell you more yet. But a man supposed to come and see me. After he come, I will have more to say to you.

(Kosh and Tonne exit. Drums. Enter Kontè who sings a slow rhythmic slow song then continues the story.)

Prologue

KONTÈ

I was beginning to get worried. You see I never trusted Kosh although he and Tonne come from one. Kosh was always impatient. Never could take his time with anything. And always running from Djiné culture. He stay close to the priest with only money and power in mind. Then when his wife join Pentecostal, he join that too. Always wanted everything quick, quick, quick so whenever Kosh said he had a plan, I knew it was the beginning of trouble. You see, one day Tonne's wife become very ill. Stroke doctors say, but I knew better. The lady was always all-right. Then one day she fall down, bodoop. Couldn't walk, couldn't talk till she pass away. Jealousy! Kosh wife is a very jealous woman and never like the fact that Ma Tonne was the one in control. She had to put her down. Tonne shoulda never, never let that woman put one foot in his house. But he always thought that his family and Kosh's family should be one. But some people are greedy, they always want to have more and that is the problem with Kosh and his family. When Tonne wife fall sick it hit me hard but Tonne is still a lucky man. He have a good daughter, Sandra. Strong, and full of determination.

ACT ONE
SCENE ONE

(Drums play a rhythm for dancing. Sandra leaps unto the stage followed by five other dancers. As they finish the dance, Garvin, one of the drummers goes to hug Sandra.)

SANDRA

You like it.

GARVIN

I love it but it is not quite ready yet.
(as he moves over to Sandra, the dancers stretch and loosen)

SANDRA

You said you love it. Why you making me wait?

GARVIN

I want more.

SANDRA

No. What do you mean it is not quite ready?

GARVIN

A little more rehearsal that's all, to get a little more balance.

SANDRA

I'm ready, Garvin.

GARVIN

I'm trying to see.

SANDRA

(dismisses the dancers with a hand signal)
I have a solo piece that is ready. I want a chance, Garvin. You said you would talk to the entertainment manager at the hotel for me. Doh mess around. I can dance. You can see that.

GARVIN

I know but I see more than that.

SANDRA
I need to earn some money. I'm trying to train the dancers so that eventually we can have a whole dance troupe. Things are getting worse on the estate these days. All the men are leaving the bananas. Daddy's not even in it like before.

GARVIN
I'd love to see your piece.

SANDRA
I think he's finally beginning to give up. So long I telling him that bananas gone. Now we have so much competition from the American companies in Latin America. They producing bigger and better bananas than us. I try to explain that to him. It's no use. We have to try something else. Where is your drummer?

GARVIN
Zanji?

SANDRA
Yes.

GARVIN
I will do the drumming.

SANDRA
You cannot, it's a *Bèlè Kont*. When I try all these modern dances, you tell me I eh ready yet. I sticking to my roots.

GARVIN
You miss your mother?

SANDRA
She is always here, Garvin. I speak to her and I can hear her respond. Before she died, I spent so much time with her. When I went to see her, I say "Mama, this is me, Sandra." She would open her mouth and say "Ah-hh." I would say, "Mama, give me your hand," and she would give it

SANDRA (continued)

to me. Then I would take her hand into mine. It was so frail, but still so soft and warm. It was so hard seeing her that way, Garvin. Mama was so dedicated to us that she kept herself back. When Uncle Kosh was away she took care of his family. Auntie Meredith used to drop Natasha by us for Mama to take care of all day and when she come from work, is by us she used to eat. Sometimes we wouldn't see Auntie Meredith until nighttime. And Mama had all her own business to do. She had to help Daddy in the bananas, cook for all the workers. But now, look what happen. Since Uncle Kosh come back and been trying to take over the property, Auntie Meredith and Natasha band up with him to see how they could squeeze us.

GARVIN

You know they will always work with him.

SANDRA

Yes, but they should remember mama and all the sacrifices she made. All the time she was their servant. I doh want to be anybody's servant Jacob; where they just use you and chock you in a corner when you old and dry and all your energy gone. They treated Mama just like they treat the land.

GARVIN

I'm sure your mother did what she wanted, Sandra. You were her life, you, your father, all of you. Let me shout Zanji.

SANDRA

Zanji is the man. Where is he?

GARVIN

He is the man?

SANDRA

He knows the traditions. Liming by the hotel corrupt you already.

GARVIN
So why you want to come in it?

SANDRA
I need the money. It'll help me with bus fare and lunch for school.

GARVIN
Fine. I just don't want to hear you blaming the politicians when they spend money on tourism.

SANDRA
You like politics too much. I wouldn't be surprised if they buy you just now.

GARVIN
I'm sure I can make a difference.

SANDRA
Well go ahead, jump into it. Take care the sharks doh eat you.

GARVIN
I'm a born swimmer. I would run the next elections if I had the money. I am no loser.

SANDRA
You mean you would go in it to make some money.

GARVIN
Yes, I know that's what you think of me but you're wrong. I would need money to run the campaign, invest in T-Shirts, posters, host barbecues, blockos, sponsor community events.

SANDRA
That is what you would go into politics for.

GARVIN

That is what I would do to get into parliament. I would also have to dish out money to all those people who would be coming after me. All those mothers abandoned by fathers who eh feeding their children. All those lazy good-for-nothings, smoking marijuana on the block.

SANDRA

Why would you give them money?

GARVIN

I'd need them. They are the ones who'd carry the speakers and chairs and so on for meetings. It is they who would climb the ladders to stick the poster and the banners.

SANDRA

Wait a minute you're serious about this.

GARVIN

The Prime Minister asked me himself.

SANDRA

What you told him?

GARVIN

Said I would think about it.

SANDRA

How you could be such a hypocrite? You who are so critical of the government.

GARVIN

I have not been critical of the government. I am an agriculturist. I am tied to the farmers. I haven't been very happy with their privatization of the banana industry, that's all.

SANDRA

So why would you join them.

GARVIN
This is my government and they know how I feel.

SANDRA
And they accept that?

GARVIN
This is a democratic party. If I go in there, I can help the farmers. That is why they offering me to run. They know where my heart is. Maybe you should help me help them, then you can get a scholarship.

SANDRA
This baby here not for sale. If they want my help to mobilize the youth, then I have a service that they can pay to receive.

GARVIN
(playing the drum)
How much is your service?

SANDRA
Just leave me out of the politics. I am a dancer with a father who is convinced that there is some evil crawling over the land. I am not going to be like my mother, sacrificing myself for man. She should have been a dancer. I doh know why she held herself back. She was a woman of great passion. I know that. Yet she never expressed it.

GARVIN
Maybe she gave it all to your father.

SANDRA
You think he would deserve that?

GARVIN
Isn't that how you made your grand entrance?

SANDRA

Garvin, you are original. Somehow your mind always finds itself back to its origins.

GARVIN

Wow!

SANDRA

You asked for it? Now be attentive let me show you what I have to offer.

GARVIN

We'll be standing at attention, your highness.

SANDRA

We?
(She sings then dances. Garvin applauds)

GARVIN

Good. That's what I like about you, Sandra. You like to express yourself.

SANDRA

I will always say it how I see it. We have so much crime everywhere now. Look what's happening. So many youths leaving the land. Everybody seeing for themselves. Everybody looking to see what they can grab. The green gold gone. Every week some of them would get three or four hundred dollars in their pocket just for carrying bananas, now they cyan get anything. And they so angry, they want to rob everybody that have more than them. These are the problems that I want to see addressed. Who cares about us? All that trouble depressing me. Look now it reach right on our land.

GARVIN

Land and property does always bring trouble. Boundaries mean division. Doh worry too much about it. I'm sure your father and Kosh will work something out. Remember they are brothers.

SANDRA

I wish I could think positive about that. I have to go now. It is getting late. I have to go check on Papa.

GARVIN

Okay, baby.

SANDRA

Listen, leave me outta this politics. If you want to help, talk to the manager for me.

GARVIN

Okay I hear you loud and clear. Now come give me some love.

(She goes to him and they embrace.)

SCENE TWO

(Meredith, Kosh's wife, is washing and packing bananas. Enter Kosh.)

MEREDITH

Where you was since morning? Where the rest of the bananas? Why you not bringing them down? Come and help me pack.

KOSH

Where Natasha? Why you doh get her to help you?

MEREDITH

Natasha? Since when? You know better than that.

KOSH

Is you raise her that way.

MEREDITH

Yes, every problem is me. That is man. Everything that go wrong, they just blame it on woman.

KOSH
Because you all woman doh listen, that's why.

MEREDITH
Ki sa-an. Fanm sé ti-mamay non?

KOSH
From the time she small I telling you let her help you. But you didn't want her in the bananas? What is she doing now? Dressing up every day and going to town.

MEREDITH
Kosh, Natasha is twenty-four years old. She is a woman. She know what she want. When I was that age I didn't have no choice. Although my belly was big up to my throat with Michael, I was still washing and packing the bananas. And I did the same thing when I was pregnant with her and the two before her. Natasha is a girl with her own way. She want to be a aristocrat.

KOSH
That's why she dressing up and going to town so and you not telling her nothing?

MEREDITH
I have nothing telling her. You see me going to my church and she not coming. She is your daughter, if you speak to her you will know what's in her mind.

KOSH
Nothing she should have in her mind but to make use of her education. I tired of telling them that. I doh have but they should get. That's why I work hard to send them to school.

MEREDITH
She want to be on TV, Kosh, in the movies. She taking acting classes. That's what she say.

KOSH

What is that? Acting classes? I doh understand anything in that. She wasting her time.

MEREDITH

You make no sense, Kosh. I try my best to bring her up in the church. She didn't stay in it. What about Michael? He went to the community college, to the big school on the hill. Where him now? He turn rasta. I doh know when last I see him. You will blame me for that too.

KOSH

Who else?

MEREDITH

You doh see is your side of the family that have the problem. Look at Garvin . A big agricultural man he is, with university education. Big respect. If your children restless, is because they take it by you. Cyan stay one place.

KOSH

My side of the family have problem? I restless? Woman you full of mepwis, yes!

MEREDITH

Come and help me pack the bananas, Kosh, while we talking.

KOSH

I finish.

MEREDITH

What?

KOSH

Doh play like you eh hear me. Is not now I telling you that I finish with bananas. We cyan even pay the bank for the house! Is not like before. They only talking, talking, talking. They not doing nothing to help us.

MEREDITH

Kosh how you could finish with it when you eh have nothing else to do, eh tell me. You cyan finish with it until you have something in it place.

KOSH

Tell that to the government.

MEREDITH

Stop putting your mind on the government. I doh care two damn fig about the government. Is you and me I talking about. You too concern about the government. You think politicians really care about poor people? No way. They only care about winning elections. That is all they care about. They seeing for themselves, let us see for ourselves.

KOSH

They doh want the bananas. They want the money that it can bring that is why they only talking about it. But they not giving it any support. Look at how the leafspot killing our life. I finish with the bananas, I telling you that. From today I putting down my cutlass. I make up my mind. Look all about. Almost everybody around here leave the fields already. What we still doing in it? Look! I gone back in the house and rest my head. I have something else in mind that we could do before we end up on the road. When you get some sense come let us talk about it.

MEREDITH

If they going to seize the house, then is better we just leave the country. Things too hard here. We not making no money. If we cannot make money what's the use. I only happy when I in church. At least when you was in New York you use to send money. All the time I was begging you to send for us.

KOSH
I doh like New York. Not too stay. I din raise up in all that noise and confusion. For me it was just to work, make some money to build my house- a house for you and the children and come back.

MEREDITH
Yes, but look now the bank want to take the house. We have to get out from here before we end up in shame.

KOSH
I never expect that bananas would end up in so much trouble.

MEREDITH
You din expect it. Mr. Compton din expect it either. But it happen. Bananas in trouble and now everybody *bazoudi*.

KOSH
Is the politics. Too much damn politics spoiling everything.

MEREDITH
Look Natasha coming.

(Enter Natasha)

KOSH
Who say I want to see her?

MEREDITH
Natasha, your father was just asking for you.

NATASHA
Hi Dad, hi Mom.

KOSH
Somebody paying you for modelling in the Castries sun, Natasha?

NATASHA

I wasn't modelling, Daddy, I was taking your friend around.

KOSH

Friend? What you talking about?

NATASHA

Monsieur Laroche. He came to look for you here this morning.

KOSH

Henri Laroche? You sure you know what you saying? What he look like?

NATASHA

A white man.

KOSH

He reach.

MEREDITH

Who he?

KOSH

Laroche.

MEREDITH

I know. But who is Laroche?

KOSH

The same one, Laroche, whose father I use to work for. Is he who want to buy the land from us.

MEREDITH

...of the Laroche Estate...there?

KOSH

Yes. Same one. Henri is the young one. He is a big man now but I know him as a lil boy. You should know who his grandfather was? He was the man who owned all the land here.

MEREDITH
Where?

KOSH
The other side of Grande Sable

NATASHA
So how you come to own this side.

KOSH
I tell you the story already. My father great, great…

MEREDITH
…great, great, g..r..e..a..t, grandfather and so on use to work for the Laroche people and work a djès on the man… force…. him to give him part of the land.

KOSH
What djès you talking about?

MEREDITH
I grow up hearing the story. Everybody know it. How the old man Joseph who was a boss on the Laroche Estate wanted a piece of the estate. That same piece we and your uncle Tonne living on. He talk to old Laroche about selling it for him but the old white man refused. Soon after that things started happening.

NATASHA
What things?

KOSH
This is l'histoire, storytelling. Doh listen to your mother.

MEREDITH
Doh deny the truth, Kosh. Face it so that you can start coming to church. Djiné people does practice black magic.

KOSH
We worked for them. My whole family. I cyan finish know.

KOSH (continued)

My father, grandfather, great-gran...way back. Our family was the Nèg Djiné. We were always a proud people.

NATASHA

What things?

MEREDITH

Things?

NATASHA

You say things started happening.

MEREDITH

At night the old Laroche started hearing noises on his house, especially during the time when the Djiné started beating their drums and drinking their blood. They say one night in the middle of all the drums old Laroche wife just die just so. Then the old man's son commit suicide. But they say as soon as old Laroche sign the papers and give the land to old man Joseph, everything was okay.

KOSH

I *di kwik*...?

MEREDITH

Kwak! You cannot deny it, Kosh. Sell the land and let's get out of this place.

KOSH

You serious?

MEREDITH

Sell it, I tell you. Dis place curse. What they have for us here? They have no money in the bananas. To make it worse everyday is a crime, a murder, a shooting, a this, a that. I doh even feel safe going out of the house. What we staying here for? Sell the damn land.

KOSH
Is not so easy. Mr. Laroche want to buy that whole piece there, from the big Mango Palwi tree on the hill going all the way down the hill to Grande Sable.

MEREDITH
So?

KOSH
Most of that part is on Tonne side. You know that.

MEREDITH
It belong to you too.

KOSH
Tonne have the most.

MEREDITH
If we sell the part near the coast there, Tonne could still stay on top the hill. You want to give up before you try. How much Laroche want to pay for the land?

KOSH
Plenty.

MEREDITH
Plenty, what is that?

KOSH
Plenty, plenty money. You know what I mean.

NATASHA
Is he a millionaire, Daddy?

KOSH
Must be. He went to the states after his father died. So that must be…how old are you? Yes, that must be more twenty years now. His family own that other part of Grande Sable. Old French family, I think. Is them we used to work for. His

KOSH (continued)
father used to be my boss. You won't know him. He die just before you born…same year. I remember his grandfather too. Tall white man. Used to smoke a pipe. My father used to work for him. That was before bananas. They plant everything on that estate. Cocoa, limes. Old Laroche used to walk around the estate like a giant.

NATASHA
If you sell the land maybe I could go to acting school. Work for the big screen. Go to Hollywood and everything, dad. Finally make you and mom proud. What you say?

KOSH
Spend more money on school again?

NATASHA
This time it would be different dad. I would become a professional. Make plenty of money to take care of you and Ma.

KOSH
Think of taking care of yourself, Natasha. I can take care of your mother.

MEREDITH
What else the man say?

NATASHA
He coming back tomorrow morning about nine o clock.

MEREDITH
Good. Kosh, that man come all down here. What answer you have for him. It is time you talk to Tonne straight. Send a message that you want to talk to him. Bon! I finish for the day. Natasha, just come and help me put these boxes away then I can go get some rest too.

NATASHA
Me lift up boxes?

MEREDITH
Come child. You not in Hollywood yet and you will never reach anywhere if you doh learn how to sweat.

(They exit.)

SCENE THREE

(Tonne is sitting on the bench. Enter Sandra. In the background voices softly singing a melodic, mournful folk song accompanied by drums.)

SANDRA
Good morning, papa. How you feeling today?

TONNE
A little better. I see some brightness, a little sun on the banana fields but it didn't stay for long.

SANDRA
Everything will be okay, papa?

TONNE
I doh know. Is de evil curse.

SANDRA
What you mean? What evil curse? A curse on our family?

TONNE
We have to protect ourselves from that curse.

SANDRA
What curse, papa? If we doh know what it is, how we can reverse it.

TONNE

I know what it is. I remember the night before your mother get sick. I was out in the front of the house. Your mother was inside in her room preparing herself for bed. It was very quiet. The moon was full and the light had a nice shine on the banana leaves. But I sense something was about to happen. The dogs start barking like something was troubling them, but nobody was around. All of a sudden my skin feel cold. I looked up. The moon was sliding behind a cloud. The wind get stronger. Then the place went pitch black.

(He pauses.)

It was then that I see it.

SANDRA

What?

TONNE

A ball of fire, bright and rolling pas' right over the house. I hear your mother scream. I rush inside just as the moon come out of the cloud. But it was too late. Your mother was lying down on the bed. Across so. Her two feet hanging down. Her eyes closed. I shake her n' shake her n' shake her n' shake her and call her name, "Agnes, Agnes, Agnes," but she wouldn't move or say anything. I look at her. Her chest was moving up and down so I know she was still alive but her body was different. She looked dry. I could see her bones, then she just seize.

SANDRA

That's when you woke me up.

TONNE

Yes.

SANDRA

Papa, what you want me to say? You know I don't believe in those things. The doctors say that mama had a stroke.

TONNE
There is a name for everything. Yes. If is a stroke, I know what it was that strike her because I was there.

SANDRA
But you say is a curse that has to be lifted. How we going to lift it.

TONNE
We must go back to what we lost. What they tell us was evil, when the real evil is the soucouyant of greed that is sucking the life out of everything. But we must not make it worse. You must stay away from Kosh and his family. And don't forget that that boy Garvin is Meredith's brother. Do not make much with them and don't tell them our business.

SANDRA
Garvin is alright, Papa.

TONNE
He is one of them.

SANDRA
He is helping me.

TONNE
Helping you?

SANDRA
To find a job at the hotel.

TONNE
Like him?

SANDRA
He doesn't really work in the hotel, Papa. He teaches at the College. And he is an agriculturist. He buys food and fruits from the farmers for the hotel. He knows the manager well. That's how he can get me a part-time job.

TONNE
No!

SANDRA

Is a part-time job, papa. I need money so that I can finish school. If you didn't dislike him so much maybe he could help you too.

TONNE

I doh want nothing from him! Part time? Working in the hotel can never be part time. Once you step in there they take your soul. What kind of job?

SANDRA

To dance.

TONNE

You can dance?

SANDRA

The same dances I learnt from you and mama and granny. The Bèlè Konte, the Débòt.

TONNE

They will not understand those dances. The dances of old. They will think you are backward. I am glad you remember them. In those days no matter what happened we come together. These people around here forget that. That is the problem. Too much greed now. Everybody want too much. They fill their house with so many things now and then stick inside with them instead of coming together. Too much American TV. In the olden days when we danced some people use to have problems with it, calling it vulgar. Now look at what they children watching. All the children dancing with half their tail outside. In the olden days, we made our own songs and our own stories. Anything that trouble us we didn't keep it inside but we would find a way to let it out so others can know how we feel. Because everybody was family. We use to free up our minds. And after that we would eat and drink and dance and sing and have a good time.

SANDRA

Why is it we doh do that anymore? It would be good. Maybe that is what we missing. Maybe that is the reason why we so selfish, why everybody just thinking about getting more and more.

TONNE

In those days we knew how to be grateful. My father was a priest in the *Kèlè* ceremony, when we sacrificed a sheep to the gods and give thanks for a good crop. The white priest use to say that *Kèlè* was evil because they wanted us to follow their ways. But in those days, we had regard for the spirits in the trees and the rivers. We had respect for them. Now we have more evil because we don't even appreciate the earth God give us. Now the gods are angry with us because we have no gratitude. We killing everything. Everybody is so greedy. If I could do better, you would not have to go dance in the hotels. I cannot help you now. The bananas not bringing much. Things hard. Somebody should help you. You're a bright girl. Your mother was a bright girl.

SANDRA

Was. She's still there. I can feel her.

TONNE

She was bright when she was young. She was better than me. She could read and write. They ask her to be a teacher. But she wanted to stay home, take care of her children and help on the land.

SANDRA

Mama used to encourage me to dance.

TONNE

I know. She liked to dance herself but her mother and father did not like it. They were light-skinned people who stayed close to the church. They were poor and worked on the land

TONNE (continued)
just like my own people but they didn't like Djiné religion. Wanted a different life for their daughter. Nothing that had to do with African people culture. I don't think they like it when she got married to a man black like me.

SANDRA
You're a good man, papa, and you worked hard. Let go of the past and look to the future.

TONNE
The future is yours, Sandra. Yours, not mine. Think about what you can do for this place. I know it is hard but you must not give up. You right to put your mind on your education but take care with this hotel business. I don't like it too much. And watch that boy Garvin . His sister is an evil woman. She was always jealous of your mother. She is a damn soucouyant hiding behind the church. I doh know what she do to take us, but I tell you I going to find out; and when I find out, it going to fall right back on her.

SANDRA
How you going to find out, papa?

TONNE
There are ways and means, old as the trees. We have to return to Ogun and Shango.

(Drum roll.)

SCENE FOUR

(The next morning. Natasha sits on the bench rehearsing with an imaginary partner.)

NATASHA

"I know you crying, but I must still talk. I see you in the field, there, you alone, planting, you and the damn mule, and I know how much you love the earth. And I wish I could love you like you love the earth. But in the war, when I was with the soldiers, even when I used to feel so shame, I know I was not for this country life. Maybe because I have their blood in me. French blood. Maybe I want all that. My life is Le Cap. But sometimes I does just feel, at my age, like an old black woman up in the mountains with my teeth going, my body getting dry and nothing to do but cook white yam and a piece of saltfish for you. You understand what I am saying?"

HENRI

(Enters unobserved by Natasha)
Parfait.

NATASHA

What?

HENRI

I understand what you are saying.

NATASHA

You were listening?

HENRI

Repeat. Say that part again about when you were with the soldiers for me.

NATASHA

Not me, Yette.

HENRI

Yette?

NATASHA

Yette from The Haytian Earth by Derek Walcott.

HENRI

Yes. You are very impressive.

NATASHA

You think so?

HENRI

Of course. That's true. You told me you wanted to become an actress.

NATASHA

Yes

HENRI

That bit I saw there. Yes, it is very impressive. If it was an audition and I was the director you would be signing a contract already.

NATASHA

I'm ready to sign.

HENRI

(taking out a notepad from his case)
Okay, Julia Roberts you get one million dollars for....

NATASHA

No, two million.

HENRI

Mon Dieu! Good. We are aiming high.

NATASHA

(Coquettishly)
Well, since you've been watching Pretty Woman...

HENRI

Ha! You're smart. So what are you working on?

NATASHA

I am actually auditioning for a part in the play. The audition is tomorrow so I was just rehearsing my lines. You're here to see my father, of course. Let me get him for you.

HENRI
Hey, don't rush off on me. Look, I brought you something. Just a small gift to show my appreciation to you for showing me around yesterday.

(He withdraws a small parcel from his bag which he hands to her.)

NATASHA
That is very kind of you sir.

HENRI
No, no, no, you were the one who was kind to walk around in the blazing sun with me. Now open it.

NATASHA
(She opens the parcel.)
A chain! Gold! Wow sir, that's too much. That must be expensive.

HENRI
Let me help you to try it on. Fantastic!
(looking into her eyes)
You are so attractive.

NATASHA
Let me go and get Daddy for you.

HENRI
Okay, I am waiting here. *Cette une belle vue*.

NATASHA
Yes. That's what we call here.

HENRI
Belle Vue!

NATASHA
I always liked here. As children we use to follow the elders here. This was the centre. Any special occasion and we would find ourselves here. Birthdays, weddings, funerals.

HENRI
Interesting. And you danced?

NATASHA
Danced and sang. This was always an exciting place. I can still hear the drums. Can you hear them?

HENRI
The drums? (strains to listen) Wait, I am listening, No I must confess eh, I am not hearing them.

NATASHA
I always hear them. I feel them all around. They seem to come from under the ground. Mama stopped dancing when she joined the Pentecostal church but she couldn't stop me from stealing away. We used to dance so much.

HENRI
Used to? You don't dance anymore?

NATASHA
We still dance the Solo and the Kont late in the year, in October and November. If you're here long enough you will be in time for some.

HENRI
I know them.

NATASHA
Yes?

HENRI
Belle Vue of the mountains. Belle Vue of the sea. It is full of beauty here. Like you. You don't know what you have here. I like the energy in the waves, the big ones.

NATASHA
The breakers.

HENRI
Breakers. I like to see it at night. Where is the road to the beach?

NATASHA
Come. Look between those two coconut trees just across that road there. The track begins right below them and leads through that coconut plantation that you see there. Once you follow the track straight through, eventually you reach a large mangrove swamp.

HENRI
I remember.

NATASHA
Soon after that, you would be under some almond trees and right on the sand.

HENRI
It is not so close.

NATASHA
We used to walk down there all the time.

HENRI
Yes.

NATASHA
But it's not exactly a beach. It's very, very rough. My father still keeps a canoe down there that he lends to the younger fishermen. The same canoe, that he used to go to Martinique the first time. Sometimes when he gets very upset with Ma, he threatens to go on the water but I know it is just a threat-he isn't mad.

HENRI
(aside) I'm not too sure about that.

NATASHA
Excuse me.

HENRI

I want to be sure of that. You and me, can we down there one day?

NATASHA

I hardly go down there anymore.

HENRI

Scared?

NATASHA

A little.

HENRI

Black magic?

NATASHA

There are spirits down there. Many spirits. Spirits of the Nèg Mawon. Spirits of the Djiné. Spirits of the Amerindians. The spirits live in the mangrove.

HENRI

Spirits of the French.

NATASHA

Who will talk for the British?

HENRI

I do not care about the British. Let us go down. Don't be scared. You're intelligent and educated. D'accord?

NATASHA

Yes. I'm educated enough to know about the Black Caribs and the wars they fought down there defending the land against the colonialists. It is said that bands of them threw themselves from the cliffs instead of surrendering to the slave masters. Their spirits are still alive and they are angry. Sometimes at night if you listen carefully you can hear their cries.

HENRI
Interesting. Good stories for tourism.

NATASHA
The sea is very, very rough down there and the wind howls at everything.

HENRI
Good for surfing you think?

NATASHA
It all glitters for you don't it? Yes; excellent for surfing.

HENRI
Just what I thought.

NATASHA
You really are interested in buying the place, aren't you?

HENRI
Your father tell you, oui?

NATASHA
That's all he could talk about. You have your own magic. You sure put a spell on him.

HENRI
Can I put a spell on you too?

NATASHA
And send me to acting school, maybe.

HENRI
You're sharp. Your father talks about you all the time.

NATASHA
Yes?

HENRI
He used to worry about you, I think. I know the reason why now. You're so attractive.

NATASHA

Yes, he gave me countless lectures over the phone. "Put your mind on your school work, Natasha. Don't let these foolish men fool you and make you pregnant, eh! You hear what I tell you. Do something with your life." Well, I finished secondary school, went on to do A'levels, didn't get pregnant.

HENRI

Congratulations!

NATASHA

I think he is still disappointed in me though.

HENRI

Why?

NATASHA

Doesn't understand what I am doing. He would be much happier if I was sitting at a desk in some office somewhere or working in a bank, counting money.

HENRI

Yes, Natasha. You're right. I want to buy this place. Let's walk down to the sea and I can tell you all about it.

NATASHA

Now?

HENRI

It's a beautiful day. I need to have a clearer picture, you know, get a closer look at this mystery of the mangrove. Ah history, what we have lost!

NATASHA

What do you mean?

HENRI

L'histoire. This should have been a French island. Ah, 1794!

NATASHA

1794?

HENRI

Yes, that is when the French and the Nèg Marron come together in these mountains. After the French under Sonthonax and Polverel had abolished slavery.

NATASHA

Right! After the French was forced to abolish slavery.

HENRI

Forced?

NATASHA

Yes. Remember after the uprising in Saint Domingue, Haiti. It was chaos. The revolution was spreading in all the colonies, even here. They had no choice.

HENRI

Ah, *tu lis ton histoire, aussi?*

NATASHA

Ah oui. Napoleon Bonda plat.

HENRI

Bonda plat. Good one.

NATASHA

We had this little song we used to sing at school.

(He joins in the chant.)

NATASHA AND HENRI

Napoleon Bonda plat.
He went to school on a donkey cart.
The donkey let go a Russian fart
That split Napoleon's balls apart.

HENRI

(laughing) Ah now that is not very nice, eh. Yes. It is true. Napoleon send troops to the Caribbean to re-establish slavery. They had success in Guadeloupe.

NATASHA

But not in Saint Domingue. You see we are strong. The play that I am rehearsing with Yette. The Haytian Earth by Derek Walcott. That is what it is about. The Haitian revolution.

HENRI

Haiti should have stayed with the French. Now she has so much poverty and voodoo. But enough about Haiti. Let us think about St. Lucia, about Belle Vue and the difference I can make here.

NATASHA

Don't be scared of the voodoo.

HENRI

I'm not scared of anything.

NATASHA

No?

HENRI

No.

NATASHA

My Uncle Tonne is a *Kèlè* priest.

HENRI

The *Kèlè*.. I remember…vaguely…

NATASHA

A ceremony where they sacrifice a sheep to Sango and Ogun and drink the blood.

HENRI

I know…voodoo.

NATASHA

It's a religion my people brought from Africa.

HENRI

I know it. It always seem to happen some distance away. Down by the river. We were never allowed to go there. Bad stuff, my father used to say…*magie nwè*, evil stuff. But like you I was always drawn to the drums and the voices. Listen forget all this voodoo talk and let us walk down to the beach.

(Enter Kosh)

KOSH

You just reach and you go straight into adventure.

HENRI

Man. Kosh. Good to see you.

KOSH

Same here.

HENRI

You look the same; in fact, younger. Is all this fresh air and good food, right?

KOSH

You yourself look as clean as a coin, Henri. Since when you here? How come you didn't tell me you coming?

HENRI

Come on man, you know that I was coming.

KOSH

Yes, it's true I know you had to come but you didn't say exactly when.

HENRI

It does not matter. Natasha welcomed me. She is very pretty.

KOSH

She take a lot by her mother side.

HENRI

Must be true. So how are talks going on with your brother? Is he coming around?

KOSH

I come to meet him here right now for us to talk.

HENRI

Well Natasha here was just showing me around, getting me into the right spirits. So go talk to your brother and when we come back you and I can have a proper chat. Does that sound okay?

KOSH

I think I see him coming. Let me talk to him alone.

HENRI

Make it good.

(Exit Henri and Natasha)

SCENE FIVE

(Kosh at banana shed, waiting. Tonne enters.)

TONNE

You send a message saying you want to see me.

KOSH

I have good news for you my brother.

TONNE

Since when you call me brother.

KOSH

We are brothers.

TONNE
I not saying no.

KOSH
You can be a rich man, Tonne.

TONNE
To be wise is to be rich. What it is you want?

KOSH
A man is here, Tonne. A man loaded with money. He wants to give us three million dollars for the land.

TONNE
No.

KOSH
You did not hear me, Tonne. Three million dollars!

TONNE
Which land?

KOSH
Our land. Belle Vue. From here, right where we stand, down to the coast.

TONNE
You mad.

KOSH
Is true. But you would still have a piece.

TONNE
What piece? Go in peace, Kosh.

KOSH
The piece on the plateau, where you raising the pigs, Tonne.

TONNE
That is not enough for our family. You serious? That is the plan you say you had? We cannot sell all that land. To sell

TONNE (continued)

that land means to sell the river, to sell all the campeche, the mangue, to sell our soul. You are mad, Kosh.

KOSH

Three million dollars, Tonne. Imagine. Your life will change.

TONNE

My life not changing now at my age. Let everything around change. Why the man want all our land? That land that come down so many generations. I was neither a stone nor a seed then. You and I did not pay for the land. Why we must sell it? Our great great-great grandfather, I not even sure how many greats, used to work on the land for the white French people. He sweat and burn in the sun, save his money to buy it from them. Is so we get thirty *carrées* of land. They leave it for us. Is sell we going to sell it, just so?

KOSH

What you going to do with the land, Tonne?

TONNE

That is a foolish question. What about the children? You were not happy that Papa and Mama did not sell the land? What about our children? And all the other grandchildren from Pa side? *Ki legitim, ki bata*! They should be happy to get the land too. Tell me, what about them?

KOSH

The lazy useless ones that smoking weed and playing rasta?

TONNE

What we going to do? Chase them like wild goats because their father, our brother, did not go to church with their mother. Where will they go? And what about our own children?

KOSH

Who tell you the children want land?

TONNE
Who tell Mama and Papa we wanted land? Uh? Answer me that? You were not even born yet when they say the land was yours. You had no use for it then. You were not happy for it then. When you turn big man you was so glad to get it.

KOSH
We can use the money to help the children.

TONNE
Now when the money finish, what happen? Answer me that, Kosh. Money does finish and what happen when it finish?

KOSH
Is three million dollars between the two of us, Tonne.

TONNE
Is not between the two of us. We will have to share it with everybody in the family.

KOSH
It would still be a lot of money.

TONNE
No matter the size of money it can finish. And when it finish, we will have no money, no land. You will be on your backside, Kosh.

KOSH
You are always a foolish and stubborn man, Tonne. You are backward. You want to remain in the backward life of the Djiné.

TONNE
I am proud of my roots and I am sticking with them until the almighty take me away. If I was not stubborn you and your wife sell me too.

KOSH
That is the problem too. Your family never like my wife.

TONNE
You like her?

KOSH
What kind of question is that?

TONNE
You don't realize it, Kosh, but I will tell you. You always looking for an excuse to run away and you doh even know why. Is your wife. Is she you looking to run away from. That woman is wicked. And a schemer. You looking to sell the land. If you do that, she will take all the money from you.

KOSH
You are a backward man, Tonne. I will leave you alone. Goodbye.

TONNE
(As Kosh leaves.)
Go forward Kosh but I tell you it will be too late for you if you chop down your own roots.

(Drum Roll.)

SCENE SIX

(Garvin is waiting. Enter Sandra.)

SANDRA
What the boss-man say?

GARVIN
Messieurs, girl, give a man a break, nah. You cyan even say 'good evening, Mr. Handsome. How good it is to see you?'

SANDRA
Good evening, Mr. Handsome. Is it good at all to see you?

GARVIN
Too late, it's false.

SANDRA
Suit yourself. Tell me the news. The big shot want our dances or not?

GARVIN
If he does, I suspect he would want them genuine.

SANDRA
Anyhow I come is original, so doh test me.

GARVIN
Not your good mornings, though.

SANDRA
How you so sensitive this morning, something troubling you or what?

GARVIN
Maybe ah just looking for some love.

SANDRA
Hey, stop getting soft on me there and tell me what de man say.

GARVIN
Yes.

SANDRA
Yes?

GARVIN
The boss say yes he will.

SANDRA
Yes!
(she jumps on him)

GARVIN
Wow! Just what I been hoping for. Stay there a while.

SANDRA
So when we starting?

GARVIN
Well you see that is the question. Before you start, this Friday…

SANDRA
(Jumping on him again.)
This Friday! Oh oh oh!

GARVIN
Ah, ah, ah!

SANDRA
(Jumping down again.)
Garvin, you are such a nasty man.

GARVIN
You wouldn't give me chance to finish what I am saying. You just getting so beautifully excited.

SANDRA
And you were enjoying it.

GARVIN
Hey what am I supposed to do. I'm trying to keep myself up.

SANDRA
Yes. Of course; I felt it.

GARVIN
Little liar you.

SANDRA
What did the man say?

GARVIN
Well I went to the hotel yesterday and went into his office. Normally I don't need an appointment. His secretary wasn't at her desk so I went in and he wasn't in either.

SANDRA
Garvin please, just skip the long story.

GARVIN
Luckily before I left, I decided to take a look at the cabaret area, thinking of you, of course. You'll never guess who I saw there, on the stage, performing.

SANDRA
Who?

GARVIN
There, looking so confident and graceful. You'll never guess.

SANDRA
I'll strangle you.

GARVIN
So confident and graceful, reciting some poetry.

SANDRA
Natasha!

GARVIN
Bingo!

SANDRA
The bitch! Don't tell me you had nothing to do with it.

GARVIN
I had nothing to do with it.

SANDRA
She's your niece, Garvin.

GARVIN

So? Listen please. Let me finish. He is seeing you on Friday. That's what I have been trying to tell you. It's an audition. That's why he was also seeing Natasha. He looking at some presentations first then he will decide which he will choose.

SANDRA

So I am supposed to compete with Natasha? I will beat her.

GARVIN

Hey, hold on. You are too ready for war.

SANDRA

These people want everything. Nothing is enough for them.

GARVIN

Come on, leave that alone. Tell me, are you ready for Friday?

SANDRA

Don't ask me to show you again. You know I am always ready.

GARVIN

I wish I was as ready as you.

SANDRA

Ready to dance.

GARVIN

That would be easy. No.

SANDRA

Ready for what then?

GARVIN

You know.

SANDRA

Today is guessing day, I see. Well guess what, today I am not in the mood.

GARVIN
What happen?

SANDRA
Daddy woke up this morning disturbed as the weather. He sat in the porch all morning looking at the sky. He must have been there from very early studying the moon. Would hardly get up. Wouldn't even eat. The only time he got up was to step out of the house to have an even closer look at the sky.

GARVIN
What did he find?

SANDRA
Please don't try to be funny. Don't forget he and Delaire was of the same family. Daddy believes in his religion. The religion of the Djiné. But since Ma has left us he getting even deeper into it. He keeps talking about the need to hold a *Kèlè* because he says that he can feel the presence of the soucouyant. Says he can feel it getting stronger and coming closer.

GARVIN
I really doh know why your father keeps up with this superstition. Holding a *Kèlè*? He must be joking. *Kèlè* died with old man Helaire. Since then everyone has forgotten about this. This is a time to be more progressive. You must encourage your old man to leave this alone, Sandra.

SANDRA
Daddy? No way.

GARVIN
We have to move forward which reminds me. I'm jumping in, Sandra.

SANDRA
Jumping?

GARVIN

In the fight, the political fight.

SANDRA

No way.

GARVIN

I'm serious. Yesterday the Prime Minister asked me himself. I told him that I would think about it and give him an answer by this evening, but I have already thought about it. You know that.

SANDRA

I know that you would sell out one day.

GARVIN

You're wrong Sandra. I want to help.

SANDRA

There are other ways that you can help. What about your work as a teacher? Isn't that help?

GARVIN

Yes, but…

SANDRA

Admit it, Garvin . You want to enter politics for the money, the power, the prestige, the highlife, the women. The same thing you were always criticizing the politicians for, you want it.

GARVIN

If that's what you want to believe, then go ahead.

SANDRA

It's the truth.

GARVIN

No. Prestige? I have absolutely no interest in that. And you never know me to be a womanizer so where is all this coming from all of a sudden? And what's wrong with having a

GARVIN (continued)

little power, Sandra? And a little more money? Maybe with some of the power and money I can help you fulfill your dream and get to university. Come sweetheart, listen I have not even won yet. I don't even know that I am going to win.

SANDRA

Why shouldn't you win?

GARVIN

Then help me and we can win. You know we make a good team. Come give me your support. Please. Come. Will you? Come closer sweetheart and stop worrying. We safe.

SANDRA

I'm not sure Garvin . I am beginning to believe what papa is saying. Maybe there really is a soucouyant out there. Maybe that is really what sucked the life out of Ma and it is coming for all of us. Maybe instead of supporting you, I really should be supporting my father to protect all of us.

SCENE SEVEN

(Kosh at the banana shed. Henri returns)

HENRI

So you talk to him?

KOSH

He was always a hard-headed bull. A *Towo*.

HENRI

I take it he doesn't agree to sell.

KOSH

I will get him, doh worry. Not me going to remain poor on this land. What use is the land if we have no money?

HENRI
What he say?

KOSH
Sakwé Kouyon.

HENRI
What?

KOSH
A damn fool he is. That's what I mean. Never pass school.

HENRI
Passed it straight, huh?

KOSH
Straight, straight, straight like this coconut tree you see there. And he was the only one who could climb that coconut tree too. That's why he so damn stupid. Eat too much of the dry ones. He want to control all of the land as though it is his. Is not his! Is mine and I will show him!

HENRI
So he don't want to sell?

KOSH
That's what he say, the jackass. That's what he say.

HENRI
There must be something we can do.

(Enter Meredith)

MEREDITH
You should talk to my brother. He know about these things.

HENRI
Where does he work?

MEREDITH
He is a big teacher at the college on the Morne. And he does advise the Prime Minister. He know a lot of the big shots in the society. In fact, he even going up for politics.

HENRI
Certainly sounds like a guy we could be talking too. When can I meet him?

MEREDITH
Anytime. He always around here.

KOSH
Fooling 'round with Sandra.

HENRI
Who's Sandra?

KOSH
My brother's daughter.

HENRI
Shucks. Sounds like trouble.

KOSH
No trouble. He is a man, well educated.

HENRI
He was her teacher?

KOSH
Oh yes! She is a woman already.

HENRI
Like Natasha?

KOSH
Natasha is only twenty. Sandra have two years more than her.

HENRI
Well, we have to talk to him if you think he can help.

MEREDITH
I will bring him to you, Mr. Laroche, and everything will fix up. You will see.

(They exit)

SCENE EIGHT

(Meredith and Garvin in the shed. Sandra is stage right, but unseen by them)

GARVIN
My sister, what you still doing here?

MEREDITH
Waiting for you, my brother.

GARVIN
Yes?

MEREDITH
You think it's a secret that you spend plenty time up there in the bush? Tell me what you see in this wild girl.

GARVIN
You still have a sting for a tongue. You know Sandra has always been close to me. So I pass to see her now and again.

MEREDITH
Now and again. From what I hear, is only a house you missing to build under that mango tree.

GARVIN
Okay, alright, so I have been spending time there. I like Sandra. She's intelligent, full of energy and ambition.

MEREDITH

And you like energy.

GARVIN

Stop teasing me sister. What do you want?

MEREDITH

When last you saw your mother?

GARVIN

Just last week.

MEREDITH

For her that's ten years ago you know that.

GARVIN

Yea, I've been busy, sister.

MEREDITH

Busy under the mango tree.

GARVIN

No seriously. I'm sure you've heard. I've been helping the party. Elections just around the corner and they want me to go up.

MEREDITH

You are going up?

GARVIN

They've asked me and actually I'm supposed to give the Prime Minister my answer this morning.

MEREDITH

So you going to tell him yes, of course.

GARVIN

Don't know. I was going to but now I don't think that I can make it.

MEREDITH

My brother, you can do a better job than most of the fellas that already there, *simen-in gwenn*.

GARVIN

I know that but that's not all. If I have to work this constituency properly, I would need support. You know that.

MEREDITH

You know that you will get our support, you know that.

GARVIN

Thanks, I would need that but I would also need some form of heavy financial backing. I am not into bluff. I want to run a different campaign, start doing some concrete work right away. No way am I just going to go on promises.

MEREDITH

Backing. That's sound like a big sum of money. Where you getting that? You doh need money. The people will believe in you. They know you. We grow up around here among them. Our father help so many people around here before he gone. He was a farmer, butcher, truck driver, everything. The people will remember that. And everybody keep telling me you're the picture of him. They will vote for you because they will also be voting for him.

GARVIN

I should make you my campaign manager. You sounding so confident, is like you work it all out already. But tell me my sister.

MEREDITH

Yes. We are brother and sister and I want to help you. There's a man who want to talk to you.

GARVIN

A man?

Act I, Scene Eight

MEREDITH

Laroche.

GARVIN

I know that name.

MEREDITH

The old family who used to own the estate. Remember these stories we used to hear how Kosh people had work a djès on the Laroche people and that's how they get the land.

GARVIN

That's it. Laroche. The last of them ran away to the states, right.

MEREDITH

Well, Kosh used to work for that family in New York. The younger one is here. The son. He have a lot of money that he want to spend. You need to talk to him. He can help you.

GARVIN

Come on, big sister, be straight with me. Is it me you really concern about or yourself. You still in trouble with the bank, right?

MEREDITH

They want to seize our house, Garvin. You know that. I told you. I doh even want to think about it.

GARVIN

Why you all build such a big house?

MEREDITH

Is not that, Garvin? Tonne and his daughter so jealous of our house and now you want to join them? We didn't have any problems with the bank. Is since things go so bad in the bananas. What we going to do? Anyway I say I doh want to think about it. Kosh have an idea. Talk to Laroche. You

MEREDITH (continued)
need money too if you going up for politics. Doh let this girl take your head. We come from a family with ambition. You can help me and I can help you. Now I will arrange for you to see the white man right away.

GARVIN
Okay my sister. You do that.

SCENE NINE

(Sandra and Tonne sits at the bench. Tonne is drawing a cross and filling each space with Shango stones while dancing ritualistically to the sound of drums)

SANDRA
What are you doing, papa?

TONNE
The signs. We have to pay attention the signs. I can feel the soucouyant getting nearer and nearer. We have to stop them Sandra. They are dangerous. We need protection. You have to watch them, my daughter and you must help me. You must help me find the right stones and carry them here, fill the whole cross - the cross directly beneath the biggest star. When the fire comes we need to contain it with the cross. If not the soucouyant will descend upon us all.

SANDRA
Fire? Stars? What are you talking about, Papa? It's broad daylight.

TONNE
No matter, Sandra. We have to draw the cross before nightfall, then when darkness falls you must help me find the cross in the sky.

SANDRA

Papa, you must stop this. I have work to do. I have to study. I have to practice my dance. Why you want to draw me into this, Papa. You know mama wouldn't want me in this. She left all this when she went to the church.

TONNE

And where is she now. Answer me. She should have listen to me and hold our roots. They got her. And look now they are trying to take you and all the land too. You must pay attention to the signs.

SANDRA

What signs are you talking about, Papa? There are no signs.

TONNE

There are plenty signs, Sandra. Signs of evil. Signs of the oceans rising. Signs of the land slipping. Signs of division. The youth have no honour and respect for life. All this are signs, my daughter. Come listen. Can you hear? Listen well even through the wind you will hear screams, sirens, wild gunshots. Signs of destruction. We're losing it, Sandra. We have no gratitude for the land, for the river, for *La Souciere*—the source of our life. We're losing everything. This is why we must return to the *Kèlè*. You must help me find the stones Sandra. They must be the right stones. Look under the coconut trees. Look feel this one. Feel its weight. Feel how smooth it is. It is shaped like the head of an axe. This will be our power and the power of Shango.

(Drums)

END OF ACT ONE

ACT TWO
SCENE ONE

(We hear singing accompanied by drums. Lights come up slowly on dancers dancing the Debot. As dancers exit Kontè enters.)

KONTÈ

I di kwi. Ah mamay-la. You see how things does happen? So Meredith done pull Garvin into a complot dere to take the land from Tonne and sell it. You see how politricks and money does mix. But Garvin doh know that Sandra overhear he and Meredith. Sandra is an honest girl. I know her since she small, I telling you. That is one young woman that not in no crookedness. From the time she hear the kind of business that Garvin and them going into it much easier now for her to go on her father's side. She change. So Garvin better watch himself because tings getting hot. De ole man insist on holding his *Kèlè*.

(Garvin and Henri enter.)

GARVIN

I've been made to understand that there's an important person who needs to see me.

HENRI

No, I am here to see someone important.

GARVIN

Oh but Sir, you are the colour of importance.

HENRI

Colour don't matter these days. It is education, money, and power. Don't be so modest, big man. I've heard your name all through the trees since I come. You are very important, I know. The way I hear it, folks around here treat you like the dictionary.

GARVIN

Wish I could provide them with more meaning.

HENRI

Heard that you mean very much to the Prime Minister and he want you to bring the seat to him next election.

GARVIN

Pardon me but in the meantime, do you mind if I take this seat.

HENRI

Do this with honour, honourable. Elections I hear, happening this year.

GARVIN

In the short time you been here you certainly are quite up to date.

HENRI

Thanks to your sister.

GARVIN

She said your name was…

HENRI

Laroche. Henri Laroche.

GARVIN

Sounds like an oil tycoon.

HENRI

Maybe, who knows? I can be anything if it would get me what I want. Just like you, honorable. I can see you are going for what you want.

GARVIN

You got it all wrong. My sister is way too optimistic. I have some stiff dishonest competition. This is my community. These are my people. If it was left to simple sincerity I wouldn't have a problem but with the emphasis now on trinkets and bluff.

HENRI
Politics is a game my friend. You have to play it. Come on, you know that.

GARVIN
Are you a politician?

HENRI
Close. Close enough to them. I know how it works. But time is short and I have to get to Dominica in the next couple of days where I am also building a resort.

GARVIN
Laroche…Laroche..Laroche…

HENRI
Lucian.

GARVIN
Old French family. Who owned this estate before…

HENRI
Before it was jinxed out of our hands.

GARVIN
Jinxed?

HENRI
You've heard the story, I'm sure.

GARVIN
So you've come to reclaim.

HENRI
You can put it this way if you like. I'm willing to pay. So let's talk business. Quick! You help me and I help you.

GARVIN
What do you want?

HENRI
I want the land from the top of the hill right down to the entire coast.

GARVIN
You're crazy.

HENRI
My bank account is also crazy.

GARVIN
Why?

HENRI
That's my business, real estate. When my grandfather migrated to New York he started buying old buildings, refurbishing them and selling them. By the time we joined him he was already a millionaire. We now have properties as far as California and Florida. It is now time for us to invest in the Caribbean.

GARVIN
We have a problem, Monsieur Laroche. Mr. Tonne, who owns most of the land, has absolutely no interest in selling.

HENRI
Maybe we can persuade him.

GARVIN
He's unpersuadable where that is concerned. You're not the first developer who's shown an interest.

HENRI
If I don't succeed with him then…

GARVIN
Then…

HENRI
That is where you come in.

GARVIN
I'm not following you.

HENRI

Patience. You see what I want to construct here is new. It's a skiing resort with a training component, a school. You don't have this here. I believe it is of interest to the government.

GARVIN

It would be. It's tourism.

HENRI

From what I hear and what I see bananas is out, tourism is in. A skiing resort is new and of special interest to the state for developmental purposes so if push comes to shove then the owner would have no choice in the acquisition...we would simply...

GARVIN

I see what you're getting at. I don't know. The owner cannot be fooled.

HENRI

You are slow to understand, Garvin. No one is fooling the owner but this is important for the entire country. So many people would benefit and of course, the owner would receive compensation. That is how I made it happen in Dominica. But I do not have time to work out all the logistics. I need a...a...a consultant, one who would be very highly paid, of course particularly if he has to run a political campaign, this would also be well financed.

GARVIN

I can tell you're very experienced in this.

HENRI

What do you say?

GARVIN

I'm thinking this is a legal issue. I'll have to discuss it with the Prime Minister and see.

HENRI
Think…ah…ah don't think too much. I leave in two days. Can't leave without an answer. One way or another. I close this project as I leave.

SCENE TWO

(Tonne sits beating a drum and reciting an African chant. Sandra is sitting next to him.)

TONNE
They want to take the land, Sandra. If we let them take it, they will take everything we have.

SANDRA
You are getting paranoid, Papa. We have laws to protect us. This is not the time of Columbus.

TONNE
My daughter, I am telling what I see and it is not good. We must prepare

SANDRA
Papa, you want me to deal in magic? You must leave it or…

TONNE
You are a damn fool, Sandra! You are not listening to me. You are listening to them when the time is coming up on us. They have their magic. You doh know that. Their priests, their lawyers, accountants, politicians all of them. All of them is t'ief. Doh let them fool you. I send you to school and encourage you to get the education that I never had, not for them to fool you.

SANDRA
They cannot fool me, Papa, but Mama taught me to believe in God, not in magic.

TONNE

You think I don't believe in God, Sandra? It is one God, the same God everywhere. Our people know God. He is growing in the trees. Hear his voice in the thunder, in the rivers. He is Shango. See him in the fire of the Sun or when the lightning is breaking in the sky. Feel him in the wind. He is Ogun, the iron in our people and our hand is strong. We work the earth and as long as we can work it, as long as this hand here can hold a cutlass, no one, no one is going to take way our land.

(Drum roll.)

SCENE THREE

(Kosh and Meredith are at the banana shed.)

MEREDITH

I doh like it. I bring her up in the straight and narrow path.

KOSH

What you doh like?

MEREDITH

What I just see.

KOSH

What is it you see?

MEREDITH

Natasha.

KOSH

What happen to her?

MEREDITH

Doh pretend you don't know. Natasha and Henri Laroche…

KOSH

I doh know anything. What you talking about?

MEREDITH

I saw them. I saw him kissing her.

KOSH

And?

MEREDITH

And what? He was kissing her. She was kissing him.

KOSH

You see them kissing. You have nothing to tell them. Yet you come and tell me. What you expect me to do?

MEREDITH

You want to tell me you didn't know nothing?

KOSH

Why me? Is how you train her. You not stupid. Natasha not stupid. She behave like a damn sheep. She just know the man, she kissing him already. If she want to kiss him, let her kiss him. Better she kiss him than kiss one of these kiss-me-arse poor boys around here.

MEREDITH

That is not the way, Kosh. That is not good in the eyes of God.

KOSH

You think I have time to worry about Natasha? She not sick. The bank want to take my roof! That's not enough for me to worry about? I build the nice big house you wanted, encourage her to stay in it. Where you saw them?

MEREDITH

In the banana shed. Look he coming.

KOSH

Just leave things alone for now. No fuss. Let's just finish the deal. Let him get the land and give us the money so we can fix our business.

(Enter Henri)

MEREDITH

Where's Natasha?

HENRI

She went to speak with her cousin. I gave her some privacy.

MEREDITH

What privacy? Sandra have nothing telling her.

HENRI

Sandra? She's your niece. Garvin told me something very interesting that Sandra told him. Her father is planning to hold that evil ceremony, the *Kèlè*.

KOSH

Where you get that from?

HENRI

Garvin.

MEREDITH

Tonne will always be an evil man.

KOSH

That is why he will never have any money.

MEREDITH

A *Kèlè*? No!

HENRI

You have to stop your brother. You cannot let him continue with this evil. *Kèlè* eh? This blood sacrifice. This is a modern world. You have to stop him.

MEREDITH

We had finish with the *Kèlè* already. Is more than ten years since the last one. The church say finish with it, is still evil. I doh know why Tonne want to do it again.

KOSH

When did Garvin say Tonne going to hold the *Kèlè*?

HENRI

Tomorrow.

MEREDITH

And we doh hear nothing about it?

KOSH

He want to keep it a secret from us, that's why.

HENRI

You cannot let him practice that evil religion on the land. You have to stop him.

(Lights dim till dark then up slowly on Stage Right for the next scene.)

SCENE FOUR

(Under the Mango tree)

SANDRA

I have something important to discuss with you, Natasha.

NATASHA

We have nothing to discuss, Sandra.

SANDRA

How can you stand here and say that? You know well they're rying to take away our land—the land of our fathers and mothers. The land of our ancestors. How can you be part of that, Natasha? How can you let them drag you into it?

NATASHA

Into what?

SANDRA

They're planning to steal the land.

NATASHA

No!

SANDRA

I overheard them speaking.

NATASHA

They're planning to buy it. You cannot call that stealing.

SANDRA

But we don't want to sell!

NATASHA

The land belongs to us-to my father.

SANDRA

Exactly! And mine. Our fathers. And because my father doesn't want to sell, they're planning to take it away from him-give him what they want for it.

NATASHA

Why you so tied to the land, Sandra? Why you so glued to this place? There is nothing here for us. No opportunities. I want to get away, go to school. Look at what is happening here. None of us is reaching anywhere. I thought you'd want the same for yourself. You think I'd want to just live my life working in town for a few hundred dollars a month. I doh know about you, Sandra, but that's not what I want for myself. Selling this land is a chance for us. Don't you see that? Tell me Sandra, what options do we have? Do you have?

SANDRA

Where is your faith? What do you believe in? You have no faith in yourself or in your roots. That was always your problem Natasha. You always wanted to be somebody else. Always wanted to be a big city girl-you grew up here but your mind was always somewhere else. That's why it so easy for you to let the land go. That's why you can be part of this *cocomacaque*-to rid us of our birth right. I shouldn't blame you, it's not your fault. It's your parents. That's how they brought you up. I can see your mind is set, Natasha. You're completely with them. I want to leave you with one warning. Just be careful that your parents are not selling you as part of the package.

(Sandra walks away.)

SCENE FIVE

(Garvin and Sandra.)

GARVIN

We have to talk, Sandra.

SANDRA

I doh know if I want to hear anything you have to say, Garvin.

GARVIN

It's very important.

SANDRA

Listen. I doh think I am interested in this hotel job anymore.

GARVIN

It's not about the job. You looking angry.

SANDRA

What do you have to tell me?

GARVIN
I spoke to the Prime Minister today.

SANDRA
My mother didn't die in vain. My mother cannot die. She's had such a long illness, and these last few months were so tough, seeing her so helpless. Now I don't even believe in death. There is no death. Death should give way to life. It is said of the Djiné peoples that they celebrated when someone died and that's what we did. That's how Daddy wanted it. And even though Mama and Daddy differed on some things I think that this is how Mama wanted it as well, that we should celebrate her life. We should create a society where the lives of everyone can be celebrated when they die. We should treasure our people and our land.

GARVIN
I spoke to the Prime Minister today.

SANDRA
There is so much mourning in our land.

GARVIN
I accepted his offer, Sandra. I'm going up next elections.

SANDRA
Up the platform? Up the ladder? To be there among the movers and shakers? For what purpose, Garvin?

GARVIN
We've been through all this, Sandra.

SANDRA
Up to yesterday I spoke to you, you were not certain. You were worried about your campaign. What you would like to do. Now suddenly everything is okay. I'll be seeing you Garvin.

GARVIN

You leaving?

SANDRA

My dancers are waiting for me. My father is waiting for me. We have to prepare. Tomorrow is an important day for us.

GARVIN

What happened, Sandra? Why are you changing?

SANDRA

I am changing?

GARVIN

Listen, you doh need the job at the hotel. That's what I came to tell you. You and your girls, you can work for me. I would need to you to dance for my launching and help mobilize the youth of Belle Vue. You know that we spoke about that. You won't have to worry about money for university anymore. I will pay you well.

SANDRA

I doh want to be part of your politricks, Garvin. Now I have to go. (He holds her by the arm.) Garvin, let me go.

GARVIN

You going to throw away all what we have Sandra. Come on, come look at me. Look at me. Can't you see. It's your father. He is poisoning your mind, turning you against me just so that he can have you support his evil.

SANDRA

Let me go, Garvin.

GARVIN

It is evil, Sandra. Blood sacrifices, pagan ritual, praying to gods nobody knows, devil worship, that's what it is.

SANDRA

Shut up! Shut the fuck up. Shut up! You call my father evil? If my father is evil then so am I and I prefer it. You hear me? I prefer that evil to all your lies. You are blind Garvin, blind and I have no doubt that you are bought. Look around you at all the suffering that is going on. It's not our religion that is causing it. It's not our culture that is causing it. It's your damn politics that's what it is. Your damn politricks and your greed for money and power. You talk about blood sacrifice. Look at all the blood that is flowing in our land. The youths that are shooting and stabbing each other senselessly. That is blood sacrifice. But look at the difference. The *Kèlè* is a sacrifice to show our gratitude to the heavens for our blessings. Your politics is a sacrifice of our people on the altar of lust for money, position and power!

GARVIN

Who are you talking to, Sandra? I am not going to stand and argue with you. You know me. You know my family. I grew up here just like you. We are of the same people. Children of the land whose parents worked hard to make a better life for them. What greed you talking about? We never know about greed. My father bought a single pick-up to transport bananas to the wharf which he drove himself. Then he bought another and hired a driver. Then he bought a minibus, then another till he was able to send me to university. That's how we do it, step by step. I owe it to my father to do the best with my life. In the days of my father, who you think occupied positions of power? Not ordinary black people. Not the children of poor people. It is my turn now, our turn. We have to take the power and see about ourselves.

SANDRA

Maybe so, but as we go for it, what are we sacrificing?

GARVIN
Come Sandra, I love you.

SANDRA
I doh know, Garvin.

GARVIN
You know that. I want you with me.

SANDRA
I doh know. Okay we see about ourselves. But what about the land?

GARVIN
Which land?

SANDRA
Stop pretending! This land here that we're standing on. What about our people and this land here of our birth? Are we losing it? I can feel that something is happening. It's slipping right underneath us like the landslides happening everywhere. And those with money and power are closing us in, further and further in.

GARVIN
It's your father, Sandra. You need to get away from him.

SANDRA
No! Let me go Garvin. Just ease the pressure. They want to kill us off and take our land. It's the *soucoyant* my father was talking about. Leave me. Go. You're on their side now. You don't have to tell me. I can feel it. I can hear it in what you are saying. Something has happened. You think I am stupid? It's that white man that you're talking to. You're not the same. We're on different sides. I believe in the almighty God, Garvin and he is not the God that is leaving our people with no hope and selling their souls into a hell of desperation. Go Garvin. Go to your politics. To your world of *bòbòl*, money and power. Go, and leave me to my fight!
(Drum roll.)

SCENE SIX

(Meredith, Kosh, Garvin, and Natasha)

MEREDITH
You have to stop him, Kosh.

KOSH
How?

MEREDITH
You have to stop Tonne from holding that *Kèlè*. What he want to do is evil and against the word of God.

KOSH
He will not hear that. Tonne have a head like stone.

MEREDITH
If Tonne hold that *Kèlè*, everything finish for us.

HENRI
Yes?

MEREDITH
Is magic, Henri, black magic.

HENRI
Voodoo!

MEREDITH
The people of Belle Vue will get involved. It will spread. More black magic. Plenty evil in the land. I doh want it! Tonne just looking for more power from the devil.

KOSH
In the olden days, it was secret. A big secret because once the priest know about it he would preach against it, but my father was a high priest in the *Kèlè*.

HENRI
How you manage to take yourself out from it??

KOSH

That is backward. The people in the *Kèlè* too ignorant. My father could not read and write. He couldn't speak English. Creole only and some African, because in his days they only had one school around here, next to the church.

HENRI

So why didn't he go there?

KOSH

His father didn't send him. It was too far from Belle Vue and besides my father had to help in the garden.

HENRI

Your grandfather was a high priest too?

KOSH

Yes. That's how my father learn. Right here at Belle Vue. All the Shango stones that Tonne using. All the tools, the axe, the hoe everything was our father own. Tonne is the one that hold his foot.

MEREDITH

You have to stop him, I tell you.

HENRI

Your family didn't do the *Kèlè*, Meredith?

MEREDITH

We not Djiné, and we not from Africa!

HENRI

Good for you.

NATASHA

We are all descendants from Africa, Mama.

MEREDITH

Maybe you, because of your father, not me.

NATASHA
You must be proud of your roots, mama.

MEREDITH
My roots are in the lord.

HENRI
But who will help your brother with the *Kèlè*?

NATASHA
Sandra, his daughter. The dancer.

MEREDITH
She leading a whole troupe of youth astray.

HENRI
Maybe somebody should talk to her.

GARVIN
(entering)
I just tried that. She wouldn't listen. She is determined.

MEREDITH
What you talking about, I thought she was your woman?

GARVIN
She's gone, I think. Her father has taken her mind again

MEREDITH
How do we stop him?

HENRI
Intrude. Spoil it!

GARVIN
That's it. You're right. Tomorrow we form one group then we all march to invade the *Kèlè*.

KOSH
Crash it.

SCENE SEVEN

(A gathering, observing Tonne stage centre. Tonne is dressed in a white robe. With him is a young man who is setting up an altar, taking the stones handed to him by another man and placing them together in the shape of a cross. Afterwards they place some yams, dasheen and calabash at the altar as well as some farming tools such as a fork, spade, a cutlass, an axe, a hoe and a rifle. There are also candles, a bottle of white rum, a mug of water, a glass, a plate, knife and a bottle of olive oil. The sound of a sheep recently washed in the river. A couple of drummers, stage right, accompany Tonne as he chants prayers. After the prayers he addresses the gathering.)

TONNE

My brothers, you do the right thing when you come to the *Kèlè*. Many will not understand but they are too ungrateful. We cannot just take from the land and not give back. We cannot just take from the land and not give thanks. The greedy ones will not support the *Kèlè*. Plenty people nowadays full of education, full of religion but they have no respect. They say that we are worshiping the devil. I do not worship the devil. I worship God almighty. Nou tout ni yon mèt. We have one master. Shango have one master. Ogun have one master. I have one master and you have one master and our master is the creator of the heaven and the earth. The ones who want to stop us. It is they who worship the devil. They destroy the earth. They take from the land when it is not ready. They take the young women when they are not ready. They poison the land. They poison the animals. They poison the water. They poison the air. How is it that they pray and destroy the good work of the creator? Who is it that they pray to? It is they who engage in devil worship. Listen to me my children I have no fear of them. The only one I fear I cannot see. I have no fear of the devil that is in them. The

                    TONNE (continued)

only one I fear is the almighty God. He makes me tremble with fear. He gives me cold sweat. My only relief is when I do his work. My only relief is when I protect his land. My only relief is when I protect the poor and the children. And I am going to protect this land from those who are trying to steal it away from us. We are going to offer a sacrifice to Shango, to Ogun, to the Almighty. We are going to sacrifice to protect our land for the children-for our children.

(Tonne kneels before the ritual objects and calls out in chant. He calls three times and after each, the drum rolls in response. During each roll he bows fully touching the ground with his forehead. He kneels in silence for a moment, takes a bottle of white rum, sprinkles some on the objects on the ground before him, three times, pours a bit into the calabash with ashes and drinks all that's left from the glass. In silence he repeats the procedure of drinking and sprinkling. The drum rolls every time he drinks. Others perform the same actions with the white rum and the water.)

Now for our sacrifice. Prepare the sheep, let us show our gratitude. Ogun, Shango!

                      KOSH

(Enters.)
No blood drinking on this land today!

                      TONNE

Watch yourself, Kosh.

                      KOSH

No devil business on this land today.

                      TONNE

I warning you Kosh before something bad happen to you. You bringing disrespect to your mother and father; to all your ancestors.

MEREDITH

(Stepping forward.)
Jesus Christ is our mother and father.

TONNE

Jesus Christ tell you to betray your people? To sell the navel of our children? Not Jesus, Judas is your mother and father.

(The sound of the goat bleating is heard offstage.)
Now let me do the business of my father. Get out of the way, Kosh and take your wife with you before you find yourself hurt. You are upsetting the spirits. I feel it.

KOSH

We not shifting, Tonne.

MEREDITH

(pushing him)
Go forward, Kosh.

TONNE

(Addressing the gathering.)
My people you see what they are trying to do? My own brother. You see how he is trying to chop the roots from the same tree that feed him. You doh know what you are playing with Kosh. You doh know. You are playing with forces, mighty and strong, forces from far, far away. Spirits that never die. Spirits that stay with us to protect us. The spirits of our mothers and fathers and of their mothers and fathers that had love strong enough to hold on to us no matter what we go through. It is when we let them go that we lose. This love I always feel, Kosh, and I will never let it go. Not for all the money in the world. I will not let it go.

HENRI

He is talking too much. The people are listening.

GARVIN

My brothers and sisters, this is not a time for us to be looking backward. This is a time for us to think about progress. This is a time for us to think about development. This is a time for us to think about employment. This gentleman you see here with us is a friend to our land, a friend to our people. Brothers and sisters, allow me to take this opportunity here today to make an announcement.

SANDRA

Sacrilegious. Disrespect. This is not the place for that.

GARVIN

Allow me to take this opportunity to let you know that I have decided to become your candidate at the next general elections.

(Some people cheer, others jeer.)
I am going to be your representative in the house and I am going to help transform this community.

SANDRA

Traitor! This is not the time or place for that I tell you. I cannot believe that you are such an opportunist. I will never let you exploit our people. Papa, go ahead with the ceremony.

(Drums.)

TONNE

Shango, Ogun, almighty creator, you who create all things, you who gave us the Sun, the rain, the rivers, and trees. You who gave us the sky, stars, the moon, and the sea. You who gave us everything. We ask you now for your power. We ask you to come down and be with us to save our land. Save us from the soucouyant. They selling our souls. They sucking the blood of our children. They selling our land. Because of their greed my father, the children are dying, the children are killing each other. They have no gratitude anymore. They are raping everything. The seas are angry.

TONNE (continued)

The fruit are sick. The animals are filled with disease yet still they cannot see. But we know that judgment will come, thunder will roll on their heads so we have no fear.

(As singers lead in the chanting accompanied by vigorous drumming, the Tonne pours some olive oil into the plate. He then takes the raw yams, makes several cross signs upon them with a knife, cuts them into pieces and then soaks them into the olive oil. Next he throws some of the yam among the objects on the ground and places some as well into the calabash. Still kneeling, he throws some of the pieces of the raw yam in the direction of the four cardinal points. Finally, he takes some more white rum and sprinkles it three times over the ritual objects again. This time he doesn't drink or sprinkle the rum and the drumming and the chanting rises into a frenzy then into silence. Three dancers bring the Sheep unto the stage. Two hold the legs while another holds out the head. They wait for the rifleman to give the signal for its head to be chopped. As the shot rings out, the sheep's head is chopped simultaneously.

Tonne stretches his cup to get the sheep's blood. As he drinks, he prays. During this time, Henri and Meredith starts slowly backing off apprehensively. Garvin and Kosh join them.)

Sandra begins a chant and dances ritualistically that scares Henri. The crowd joins in the chant picks up the farming tools, and advances to Kosh and his team intensifying the chant.)

CROWD

Run them, run them
Run them down, run them
Run them, run them
Run them down, Run them.

HENRI

(visibly frightened)
Let us get outta here!

KOSH

No!

MEREDITH

I not staying in this evil thing Kosh.
(She pulls him by the arm.)
Let us go!

(The crowd circles the stage. The chanting, movements and drumming intensify to a climax as Kosh and his party exit the stage.)

KONTÈ

I di kwi manmay-la. I di kwi! Ou wè I jonn, ou kwè sè bè. You see it yellow, so you thought was butter. Don't underestimate the power of people and their culture. Well that is the story from Belle Vue. You forget me? No don't forget me, cause is me start de story. And is me going finish it. Well, ah sure you go be happy to know that de land never sell. After that *Kèlè* Henri got too scared to continue with his plan. Poor Garvin. No big funding for his politricks. He lose de election, of course. But he still coming around troubling Sandra. Poor fella. He not giving up; but as they say, "once bitten, twice shy." It hard for Sandra to trust him again. Well, Kosh was a bit luckier. I hear he went back to Martinique to work with his French connection. That is how he manage to keep the house. Meredith? She start a church downstairs. As for Natasha, she and Sandra get close, close, close like when you see the pitons from afar. She start a doing some drama with de dancers. You ask for Tonne? He is a happy man, Right now he sitting on his balcony, deep in his rocking chair watching the dancers. Let us watch with him and give a big round of applause one more time.

(We hear the singing and vigorous drumming as dancers come on stage and dance till lights fade and they exit.)

KONTÈ

I di kwik!

CROWD

Kwak.

THE END

The Field of Power

PRODUCTIONS

"The Field of Power" was first staged at the Sir Arthur Lewis Community College in Saint Lucia on January 21, 2015, to celebrate Nobel Laureate Week.

CAST IN ORDER OF APPEARANCE

KONTÈ	Sheamain Simon and Kazia James
EVA	Brittany Henry
OLD WOMAN	Kershelle Theodore
MAWON	Reynold Cassius
BÈTAFÉ	Sherline Gittens
LADJABLÈS	Shanice Evariste
MADAME SAJÈS	Kershelle Theodore
BÒTO	Richard Ashton
SOUCOUYANT	Talis Girard
VILLAGERS	Darren Olisse
	Kameka President
MUSICIANS	Jervon Regis
	Ishmael Williams

TECHNICAL TEAM

Director and Playwright: Travis Weekes
Choreography: Richard Ambroise
Backdrop: Pablo Lucien
Wardrobe: Zenith Williams
Make-Up and Wardrobe Assistant: Marie Catty

CHARACTERS

Kontè:	The Storyteller
Eva:	a young, dark simple girl of about seventeen years old.
Old woman:	about seventy years old, dark, devout catholic.
Mawon:	Strong looking young man, about eighteen years old.
Bètafé:	Boy about 12 years old.
Ladjablès:	Very light skinned, could be white; slender.
Madame Sajès:	Hermit, about seventy years, long grey locs.
Bòto:	An old blind fisherman.
Soucouyant:	Tall, with a strong voice.
Revellers	

First Politician
Second Politician
First Salesperson ⎯ These may be played by revellers
Second Salesperson
First Vendor
Second Vendor

SETTING

A street in a fishing village in the Caribbean, set against the backdrop of houses and a track leading up to a clearing at the side of a mountain.

Upstage centre stands a wooden hut with two doors on either side, facing the audience.

In front of the door, stage right, we see a small wooden bench, a basket with a huge grater inside and beside the basket some cassava sticks.

In front of the other door, stage left, we see the seat of the Ladjablès, a big rock/stone.

A huge fishing net hangs partially on the edge of the stage(centre).

TIME

The Present.

PROLOGUE

(Music and singing begins offstage with stage in complete darkness. Lights come up slowly to bright as actors dance on to the stage. A solo voice sings the lines beginning with "*Mwen...*" while the Chorus responds "*Waya waya waya moulélé.*")

KONTÈ

Waya waya waya moulélé
Mwen moulélé mwen mouléngé
Waya waya waya mouléngé
Kote mwen pasé mwen mouléngé
Waya waya waya moulélé
Mwen moulélé mwen mouléngé
Waya waya waya moulélé
Mwen mouté au Tabour mwen mouléngé
Waya waya waya moulélé
Mwen desann Roseau mwen mouléngé
Waya waya waya moulélé
Mwen mouté Millet mwen mouléngé
He kwi
He kwi manmay-la!

(All performers, except Kontè sit in a semi-circle upstage centre. Kontè moves downstage as he begins the story.)
Is a young woman they calling Eva
living in a place called Derrière Morne
that hole on the other side of the mountain.
He kwi
He kwi manmay-la
This young woman dey calling Eva
was tired of the poverty in Derrière Morne
tired of the rum twisted faces of the men
tired of the boredom of the slow women

KONTÈ (continued)

tired of the cries of the hungry children
tired of the greed of the blood sucking Soucouyant
that dried up the bones of some
and turned them into jumbies.
Hey kwi manmay-la
Hey kwi manmay-la
So one day this young woman dey calling Eva
decide she go make a try to get out of Derrière Morne.
But the only way out of Derrière Morne
was to first go up the big mountain,
the home of the Ladjablès
where all her Fer-de-Lance hide and wait
on the side of nearly every track.
So anyone who wished to make it to the Land of Opportunity
not only had to make it through the snakes,
but also had to pass the house of the Ladjablès
who held the key through the Secret Gate.
Hey kwi manmay-la
Hey kwi manmay-la
Living side by side with the Ladjablès
was Madame Sajès, her sister by mother.
But these two sisters were as opposite as sun and rain.
Madame Sajès was a plain, quiet, simple woman,
brown as the cocoa seeds she pounded for tea.
Her sister, the Ladjablès, was the Queen of the snakes
as sly as she was loud
and yellow as the moon on a scary night.
Waya waya waya moulélé
Mwen moulélé mwen mouléngé
Waya waya waya mouléngé
Kote mwen pasé mwen mouléngé
Waya waya waya moulélé
Mwen moulélé mwen mouléngé
Waya waya waya moulélé

KONTÈ (Continued)

Mwen mouté Laborne mwen mouléngé
Waya waya waya moulélé
Mwen ay Derameau mwen mouléngé
Waya waya waya moulélé
Mwen mouté Plateau mwen mouléngé
Lajables sa-a menm!

Many men from Derrière Morne
had tried to go through the mountain.
But even those who made it past the Fer-de-Lance
were tricked into the snake dance by the Ladjablès
and swallowed under her huge net.
Few women would venture through the Fer-de-Lance,
far less make it through the Secret Gate.
But Eva, as we will see, is no ordinary woman.
Eva is a strong woman, an ambitious woman; young
but sharp and full of courage.

He kwi!
He kwi manmay-la!

One day, as Eva walked through the village
with her boyfriend Mawon,
Eva made up her mind to make the journey
to the land of the opportunity.

(Kontè sits among the villagers. Lights dim on villagers and brighten on Eva and Mawon who stand. Drum roll as Eva walks towards downstage centre.)

ACT ONE
SCENE ONE

EVA

You can get me out of here?
You? You? Any of you?
Here where no matter how I move
I cannot find my way.
No matter how I turn
I knocking my foot.
You can get me out of this cave?
Here, Derrière Morne, where our fathers crawl
in and out of the rum shops like crabs,
splashing their throats with white rum,
calling their sons, our men, to come,
disappearing into the darkness
while our mothers curse their weakness
and turn their anger upon their own children.
I want to get out of this hole, you hear me?
Take me out in the open,
take me far, far, far towards the horizon.
Let me see the ships reaching for different worlds,
let me hear the loud cry of a seagull,
to echo the cry in my dreams.
Give me a glimpse of infinity.
Pull me out of this resignation.
Pull me out of this despair.
Pull me out of Derrière Morne.

OLD WOMAN

(Lights up on Old Woman as she walks towards Eva.)
You talking for me?

EVA

I'm talking for any and everybody
but especially for myself

The Field of Power

> EVA (continued)
> and my sisters and my brothers.
> I'm talking to anybody
> and for anybody who want another life.
> Show me the way past the snakes,
> I need to get out of Derrière Morne.

> OLD WOMAN
> Not me!
> I have no wish to get out of here.
> I'm already on my way out of this world.
> The strength I have left
> is to pray for my peace.
> For my piece… up there.
> I am finished with this earth
> and all that it can give or take.
> I live a life of poverty.
> All I have are my prayers.
> That's all I have to give.

> EVA
> Give prayers? Damn you!
> I don't want to hear of it!
> You can keep your prayers
> and your poverty. You hear me? Keep them
> for your children and their children.
> I don't want it!

> OLD WOMAN
> My child… listen!

> EVA
> I will not listen.

> OLD WOMAN
> You will have to listen to me one day.
> It is not an easy journey.

OLD WOMAN (continued)

You can only get out of Derrière Morne
if you get the key from the evil one,
the key to the Secret Gate.
But you cannot fight this evil without the prayers of old.

EVA

Old Woman, I do not want to hear you.
I want someone who can help me.

MAWON

(Walking towards Eva)
Eva, do not be cruel.
Why do you want to leave?

EVA

I have explained to you over and over.
Don't I deserve a different life?
One beyond Derrière Morne,
where I can shed these rags
and have a makeover of opportunities.
Here the Soucouyant sucks all that we have
and you men do nothing but submit to his will
'til your bones get dry.
I am not cruel,
I am decided.
I have to be as strong as that mountain.

MAWON

What about my love, Eva?
What about our life here in Derrière Morne?
The house I was building for you under the breadfruit tree,
the children we spoke about who would play by the river
like we did; catching crabs and crayfish.
Are you going to break our dreams?

EVA

Our dreams of peace are already broken, Mawon
Don't you see?
The Soucouyant of the night,
lover of the Ladjablès,
has invaded our daylight
poisoning the rivers.
His cries of lust shriek in the speakers of the politician.
Turned so many of the villagers into the Fer-de-Lance,
striking divisions among family and friend.
Each one eyes the other in suspicion.
We have no trust anymore.
There is a constant clash of spirits
without any reprieve.
I can't take it!

MAWON

I will destroy the Soucouyant, Eva.
I will do it for us.

EVA

You don't have the courage, Mawon.
Why haven't you done it before?
You are too weak.

MAWON

I am kind.

EVA

Kind or foolish?
You are easily tricked.
The politicians, women,
you name it.
You fall too easily for the forked tongue.

BÈTAFÉ

(knocking his drum, rising, and walking towards Eva.)
I know the road out of Derrière Morne.

EVA

One safe from the Fer-de-Lance?

BÈTAFÉ

Safe from the Fer-de-Lance!

EVA

My little friend,
I have heard it said
out of the mouth of babes and sucklings…
Where is the road?
How can I get through?
Would you show me?

BÈTAFÉ

I will take you past the snakes,
but I will not go near the Ladjablès!

(drum roll)

MAWON

The Ladjablès!
No, Eva! You can't go.
We know the stories of the Ladjablès!

EVA

I am not scared.

MAWON

Let me go find the way.
I am the man.
Let me face the danger.
I will go and find the way
and return for you.

EVA

No!

MAWON

Why not?

EVA

Men are weak.
Yes, we know the stories of the Ladjablès.
Men are her victims.
They crumble before her power.
You would be lost.
I am the one to face her.
If you call yourself man,
stay here and fight the Soucouyant.

MAWON

I am a man, Eva,
with the flaws of my forefathers.
But I will not bow
before the cloven hoof of the Ladjablès,
neither will I be burnt by the intoxicating flames of the Soucouyant.
You have my heart and that makes me stronger.

EVA

Then prove it to me, Mawon
Stay and resist the Soucouyant.

BÈTAFÉ

I can show you the way up to a certain point, Eva.
Only up to Kayè Kabwit.
This is where I find the skin for my drum.

EVA

What is your name?

BÈTAFÉ

Bètafé.

EVA

Bètafé,
you are a glimmer of light through this darkness.
Show me the way.

OLD WOMAN

Wait Eva.
For the sake of your grandmother,
my sister in the Holy Name,
I want you to take this.
(Handing her a rosary)
Although she gave it to me
just before she closed her eyes,
it is rightfully yours.
This is the only key you need.
The key to the Field of Power!

(Drum beat.)

EVA

The Field of Power? What's that?

OLD WOMAN

The Field of Power
is the only compromise that can work for you.
It is that central place
in front of the hut of the two sisters.
Go along.
We will meet again!

(Lights fade down on old woman as she exits. Lights up as all dance around the stage. Drums and flute are played.)

EVA AND BÈTAFÉ

(Eva and Bètafé dance and sing on their way up the mountain)
Woy woy mwen vlé pati
Dibijé
Mwen ka kité
Dibijé
Ma ka manti
Dibijé

EVA AND BÈTAFÉ
(continued)

Mwen vlé mouté
Dibijé
Mwen ka pati
Dibijé
Mwen ka kité
Dibijé

(Lights dim on all as they dance offstage)

SCENE TWO

(Lights come up as Kontè enters. Eva and Bètafé mime the descriptions of the Kontè.)

KONTÈ

Hé kwi!
Hé kwi, manmay-la!
Hé kwi!
Hé kwi manmay-la!
Eva is a brave woman for true.
She and the boy climb up the mountain
and took a narrow track to the right of the waterfall.
As they pass up, Kònpè Kabwit
gave them a cut eye.
Eh eh eh eh eh eh eh eh eh eh
He kwi
He kwi manmany-la.
When they got tired and hungry
they stop under a Fwidjé tree for rest,
sitting on its giant roots.
Little Sikwyé sat down with them
chatting for a while but Mel, the blackbird

                    KONTÈ (continued)
out of jealousy flew right over them
almost biting off their heads.
Sikwiyé whispered that Mel was a bava
and would be bringing news to the Ladjablès,
so they hurry on their way.
He kwi,
He kwi manmay-la
When they reach the rock
just before the cave, they had to stop
because suddenly the place change.
The wind blow so hard
they grab unto the little trees
but the wind was so strong the trees gave up.
They had to grab Konpè Manikou's
pòwyé tree. Konpè Manikou
just running down, warned them:
"Hold on to my tree or you will be blown away.
The Ladjablès is doing her evening dance with the snakes.
If you stay here
you will be safe!"
He kwi
He kwi manmay-la!

(Kontè retreats to the wings.)
                    BÈTAFÉ
I must to go back down, Eva,
before the chickens fly to their branches
and my mother starts scratching her hair.
She says I am not ready to light the darkness,
too young to meddle with the night.
Look, the sun is turning orange
and falling behind the sea.
I must find my mother's yard
before the Ladjablès reappears
and her creatures crawl from the moon.

EVA
Wait, Bètafé, you must guide me to Madame Sajès.

BÈTAFÉ
Eva go now, you must run up this way.
Go pass the rock, straight across
'til you come to a another pòwyé tree.
In the distance
you will see an old hut,
the house of the Ladjablès,
but also that of Madame Sajès.

EVA
(hugging the boy)
Bètafé, you're the little brother
I never had. No!
You're more than my brother,
you're my guiding spirit.
My thanks to you are bigger than this mountain.
Take care…we will see again.

KONTÈ
Bètafé made mongoose down the mountain.
Eva hoped he'd be back next day, hunting for goats.
She turned to face the top of the hill
and continued her journey.
He kwi manmay-la
He kwi manmay-la
She had just reached the pòwyé tree
and seen just ahead of her
the old hut, with the thatched roof,
when just as before
the wind started raging.
Eva found herself before the hut of the Ladjablès
and witnessed her in the middle her evening dance.
He kwi manmay-la!
He kwi manmay-la!

(Drums roll and lights dim suggesting dusk/sunset.)

LADJABLÈS

(Ladjablès dances and sings. Chorus responds off-stage.)
Jab-la kwiyé mwen
Siwa-wa
Denmou kwiyé mwen
Siwa-wa
Mi mwen an bwa
Siwa-wa
Mi mwen an bwa
Siwa-wa.
Jab-la wanjé mwen
Siwa-wa
Jab-la
Denmou wanjé mwen
Siwa-wa
Ja-la wanjé mwen
Denmou wanjé mwen
Siwa-wa

(Ladjablès senses the presence of someone and spots Eva who had been spying from a distance.)
Hey you! What are you doing? Spying?

(Pulling her by the arm.)
Who brought you here? Who sent you? How did you get through?

EVA

I come in peace.
I'm searching for help.

LADJABLÈS

Help? (She laughs.)
Are you not from the dirty little village down there?
You come to me for help? (She laughs.)
I am the one that you curse? You and your mother.

LADJABLÈS (continued)

Sakwé gajé! Remember?
It was me that you curse when you couldn't find your father.
It was me your mother curse when she couldn't find her husband.
I am the one women love to blame when their men lose their way.

EVA

Of course you are to blame,
that is the very reason why I come to you.
You're the gatekeeper to the land of riches.
You hold the secrets of the mountain,
the key to the Secret Gate.
You've swallowed up so many men,
drank their power to enrich yourself,
using their seed to grow your hair,
oil your skin,
and you sit there pretty, enjoying life
while poor, young women like me suffer.
It is so unfair!

LADJABLÈS

I cannot help you.

EVA

You are so selfish.
What more do you have to gain?
What do you have to lose?

LADJABLÈS

(She laughs loudly.)
Have you come here to amuse me?
Only you can help yourself.
What do you want?

EVA

I want the way out…out…

LADJABLÈS
...out of Derrière Morne?

EVA
Yes.

LADJABLÈS
Easy. You will have to dance with me.

EVA
You…?

(Lights black, drums roll, laughter of the Ladjablès echoes all around as she leaves.)

(Lights up on Eva.)

EVA
Where are you? *Ko ou pwen, sakwé gagé!*

(Madame Sajès comes outside her side of the hut.)

MADAME SAJÈS
Life is steep, isn't it?
And scary, eh.
I told you the journey isn't easy.
Come in, come inside

EVA
No, your face.
I know your face.

MADAME SAJÈS
My face?
No, what you see here is what you think of poverty.
The un-washable stain of the coal carriers,
the image of degradation that you scorn
that you spit at.
But it will be enough for your lesson.

EVA

You… you, I know you.
I know that voice.

MADAME SAJÈS

Come spend some time with me.
I was expecting you.
Help me. Look!
I have some baskets of manioc.
So much to grate
before I make the cassava.
Sit, help me, then afterwards,
I will teach you the dances of my mother,
the ones we performed at wakes
as we honoured the spirits of the departed
then inherited their prayers.

EVA

You're crazy
I don't have the time.
How much manioc will I have to grate?
How many drums will I have to dance
before I get to the other side?

MADAME SAJÈS

An mizi, an mizi.
That is the thing.
Begin and you will finish.
Don't be too eager for the fast lane.
If you learn only the dance of the Ladjablès,
you will lose the steps of the Bèlè,
the steps and paths to our roots.
You want success but you also want to hold your own.
You must stay within the Field of Power!

EVA

The Field of power?

MADAME SAJÈS

It is that space here in the yard between her side and mine.

(She draws a circle)
Here is the circle….see.

(Eva sits down and begins grating. It is hard work. She sweats while Madame Sajès sings. Others help them perform the Gwajé Manyòk.)

LADJABLÈS

(From off-stage.)
Eva, Eva, vini Eva vini.

MADAME SAJÈS

Do not listen to that voice, Eva. It is the voice of evil.

(Eva keeps turning around away from Madame Sajès and to the beckoning voice of the Ladjablès.)

MADAME SAJÈS

I said, do not listen.

EVA

You're wasting my time. Who wants the cassava?
Old woman, haven't you heard of corn flakes?
I want the shelves with varieties of cereals from lands afar.
I need prosperity and I need it now.

MADAME SAJÈS

There are two ways out, Eva,
but both ways reach the Secret Gate.
I can show the right way.
You will have to climb all the way to the top of the mountain
then follow the track down on the right to find the Gate.
The Ladjablès will stop you as you climb.
She will try to lure you

MADAME SAJÈS (continued)
to the shorter way across through the gate,
down the side of the hill.
But that is the way through which
you will have no choice
but to dance with the snakes.
Eva, you must not give in!

EVA
(Sound of the voices. Eva turns around distractedly.)
Jab-la kwiyé mwen
Siwa-wa
Denmou kwiyé mwen
Siwa-wa
Mi mwen an bwa
Siwa-wa
Mi mwen an bwa
Siwa-wa.
Why should I trust you?
How do I know that you are the truth?
I must see for myself.

(The singing continues and she dances until she reaches
the other side of the hut. Lights up stage right as Ladjablès
appears.)

LADJABLÈS
Ah you're back, eh?
Like I knew you'd be.
Don't know why you wasting time with this old lady.
Anyone can see that she is as backward as she is black.
(She laughs heartily at her own joke)
She and I are sisters, you know. Would you believe it?
Yes, we are but we are of a different father.
My father was of a distant land, where there is progress.
A land where the voices of a people are fine like the sound
of silver

Act I, Scene Three

LADJABLÈS (continued)
and their skin and hair are the colour of gold.
My father bought this whole mountain and now that he is gone it is all mine.
(She laughs again.)
But my sister over there, that old black sack that keeps rolling in my way,
refuses to leave my territory, believes she has a claim to the mountain.
But don't let her fool you. Only I, only I can get you quickly to where you wanna go.
(She dangles a big key through her fingers.)
I hold the key to the big gate!
(She laughs again)

(Lights fade to black on Eva and Ladjablès. Drums roll.)

SCENE THREE

(Lights come up as storyteller enters.)

KONTÈ

Hey kwi manmay-la.
Hey kwi.
So while the Ladjablès tries to steal Eva's eyes,
Bètafé has made it safely to the bottom of the mountain
where Mawon was waiting anxiously
and searching for answers to defeat the Soucouyant
and the Ladjablès.
(Kontè exits quickly.)

MAWON

(Holding Bètafé firmly by the arm as he runs onstage.)
Where is she?

BÈTAFÉ

Who?

MAWON

Don't play games. Eva!

BÈTAFÉ

She is searching for happiness.

MAWON

What?

BÈTAFÉ

I left her with the Ladjablès.

MAWON

Come with me.
Let us go find answers.

BÈTAFÉ

Where?

MAWON

To Bòto, the blind fishermen,
Eva's grandfather
who, ever since he lost his eyes
is able to foresee all danger

BÈTAFÉ

He is a gadè.

(He walks over to Bòto who is untangling his net and singing. Mawon, Bètafé, and chorus off-stage join in.)

BÈTAFÉ, BÒTO, MAWON

O van vanté
O van
O van vanté
O van
Menen mwen an gwan glo
O van
Manmay bizwen manjé

BÈTAFÉ, BÒTO, MAWON
(continued)

O van
Manmay bizwen boujé
O van
Manmay kay dansé
O van
O van vanté
O van
O van vanté
O van

MAWON

Good day to you, Mr. Bòto.

BÒTO

Sh sh sh…quiet listen a moment.
The sea. The most soothing sound ever.
Listen. Hear the waves.
Always, the sea offers good wishes.
Even when it sometimes takes away the living.
It takes and it gives.
That's the rhythm of the waves.
You feel it, taking and giving,
coming and going,
living and dying.
So tell me son. What can I do for you?
How can I help you?

MAWON

My love is trapped!

BÒTO

Trapped?
I miss the freedom of the sea.
Nothing gives you a stronger feeling of freedom
than being out in the ocean.
It's a pity… my eyes….

BÒTO (continued)

Take care of your eyes, son.
You hear me?
Take care of your eyes.
Yes, tell me son. How can I help you?
Love cannot be trapped.
But you can be. Are you?

MAWON

Papa Boto. I want to tell you a story.

BÒTO

Get to the point, son.
I can see that your heart is heavy.

MAWON

It is Eva.

BÒTO

My beautiful granddaughter!

MAWON

She has grown tired of the life in Derrière Morne.
Tired of the dull shacks of poverty,
tired of the toil in the narrow streets.
She longs for the highways,
the malls, and the fancy balls.
She has left me and my farm and gone
up the mountain to seek the way to another life.

BÒTO

My son, can you blame her?
Nothing wrong with seeking a better life
Is how you reach there.
And what you do there.
And if you can find your way home when you ready.
Is what you want from the world
and how you make your happiness.

Act I, Scene Three

BÒTO (continued)

Listen! All my life I toil with my one canoe
foraging through these waters you see there,
throwing my line,
throwing my net.
Is not every day I catch.
Let Eva be about her journey.

MAWON

But is how she reach there, Papa Bòto.
You said it.
In seeking freedom,
she has entangled herself in the web of that white spider.

BÒTO

What you mean?

MAWON

She is in the home of the Ladjablès!

BÒTO

Listen my son, on this journey
all of us have to encounter the evil.
There is danger everywhere.
There are snakes here too, in this simple village.
You will never know victory
if you don't learn to conquer danger.

MAWON

But what must I do? How can I bring her back?

BÒTO

It is not up to you son.
You have your own fight here.
She has her test
and you have yours.

The Field of Power

MAWON

What is her test?

BÒTO

Her dance with the Ladjablès.

(Drum lash.)

MAWON

What is my test?

BÒTO

The dance with the Soucouyant!

(Drum lash)
The spirit of evil can take many forms.
In the mountain, it will be the Ladjablès.
In the sea it is the Denmou Lanmè.
But here in the village it comes in the form of the Soucouyant.

MAWON

The blood sucker!

BÒTO

That's it!
We cannot escape the challenge of the Soucouyant
or the Ladjablès, within or without.
We are bound to meet them one day.
Eva is a girl full of *kouway*
and you must have the same.
Always pray for *lafòs èk kouway*
and for pasyans. Very important! You hear me!
We the men of this village,
we have been failing in our duties.
You hear me? Failing in our responsibilities,
losing our way when we go to seek opportunity,
by allowing ourselves to get lost with the Ladjablès
or giving in to the temptation of the Soucouyant

BÒTO (continued)
'til our blood is sucked dry.
Look around this village.
Don't you see it, son?
You see the signs.
What is the spirit of our island?
Tell me?
Now you must face the Soucouyant soon.
Because of our weakness
we fail out families
and our children suffer.
Listen!
You hear it.
Listen carefully.
It will come after you.
Listen to me carefully.
I have been watching you.
You don't know it.
But I have been watching you and my granddaughter.
I see the two of you are in love
and I remember the days with my dear one.
Love is a good thing.
You feel it strongest
when evil beckons
your loved one.
That is the master plan.
You are a young man.
Take your responsibility.
Do not be scared.
Embrace the power of your name.
The Ladjablès and the Soucouyant are one and the same
and so you and Eva must be one.
Each of us must fight our demons.
Gather your courage and fight your evil.
No one can do it for you
but we will all be there with you.

BÒTO (continued)

Go ahead.
Listen, I hear him.
Be prepared!

MAWON

But how? How do I fight the Soucouyant, Papa Boto?

BÒTO

You must not get pulled into his net.
But even if you do, it is not the end,
it is part of the journey.
You must also hear your own songs,
the songs of the old and wise.
Even amidst the revelry of the Soucouyant,
even among his jingles and tingles
you must find the space in between.
You see this circle here?
That is your Field of Power.
As long as you stay there you will be safe.

MAWON

The Field of Power?

BÒTO

That's it. He is coming
Get ready.

(Lights dim to red. A line of revellers all under a net come dancing along the stage and chanting. They are led by the Soucouyant.)

SOUCOUYANT

Si ou paka gouté'y.

REVELLERS

Mwen épi ou pa bon!

SOUCOUYANT

Si ou paka touché'y.

REVELLERS

Mwen épi tjou'w pa bon!

SOUCOUYANT

The spirit of Saint Lucia.

REVELLERS

Drink your rum.

SOUCOUYANT

The spirit of Saint Lucia.

REVELLERS

Whole chou'w fann.

SOUCOUYANT

Si ou paka gouté'y.

REVELLERS

Mwen épi ou pa bon!

SOUCOUYANT

Si ou paka touché'y.

REVELLERS

Mwen épi tjou'w pa bon!

(The revellers emerge from under the net and assume the various roles of the Soucouyant.)

FIRST POLITICIAN

(Distributing a flyer.)
Election Day is near. Have you registered? Put your X near the Stone.

SECOND POLITICIAN

(Also distributing a flyer.)
Don't listen to him, young man. Put your X near the Rock.

The Field of Power

                            FIRST POLITICIAN
(Giving a t-shirt.)
Near the Stone!

                          SECOND POLITICIAN
(Giving a t-Shirt.)
Near the Rock!

                          FIRST POLITICIAN
(Giving a drink.)
Near the Stone!

                          SECOND POLITICIAN
(Giving a drink.)
Near the Rock!

                          FIRST POLITICIAN
(Giving another drink.)
Near the Stone!

                          SECOND POLITICIAN
(Giving another drink.)
Near the Rock!

                          FIRST POLITICIAN
(Pulling him by the other arm.)
Near the Stone!

                          SECOND POLITICIAN
(Pulling him by the arm.)
Near the Rock!

                          FIRST POLITICIAN
(Standing on a platform.)
Brothers and sisters. I will give you jobs!

                          SECOND POLITICIAN
(Pushing first politician off the platform.)
Brothers and sisters. He say he will give you jobs.
But I will do that and more.
I will put money in your pockets.

FIRST POLITICIAN

(Pushing out second politician.)
Brothers and sisters,
my party will put an end to that corruption!

FIRST SALESPERSON

(With a small box pushing at Mawon's face.)
Be mobile!

SECOND SALESPERSON

(Jumping in front Mawon.)
Be versatile!

FIRST SALESPERSON

(Pulling Mawon away.)
Don't be sorry!

SECOND SALESPERSON

Be Extraordinary!

FIRST VENDOR

Hey you!
Chicken on de grill, sah.
Eat your belly full.
Chicken is de ting, sah.
Boy, you too meg.
Come and buy a leg.
Or if you want a breast,
is me have de best.

SECOND VENDOR

(Close to Mawon's face.)
Food for your brain.
Food for your brain.
Smoke me Sensimillia
and you come back again.
Food for your mind.
Food for your mind.
Smoke de good weed.

SECOND VENDOR
(continued)

Say is me have de breed!
Say we nah make no joke
'cause we take de good stock,
'cause we raise it
and we praise it
'cause we know de right smoke.
Food for your brain.
Food for your brain.
Smoke de Sensimillia
And you come back again

(Mawon is drunk, drifting and in the midst of the confusion a Crack Sniffing Peddler offers him some crack. The Soucouyant and the others move with the net and cover Mawon, taking him along with them as they chant.)

SOUCOUYANT

Si ou paka gouté'y.

REVELLERS

Mwen épi ou pa bon!

SOUCOUYANT

Si ou paka touché'y.

REVELLERS

Mwen épi tjou'w pa bon!
Wo! Ou pa bon!
Wo! Ou pa bon!
Wo! Ou pa bon!
Wo! ou pa bon!

(They exit. Lights fade to black.)

SCENE FOUR

(Lights come up on Ladjablès.)

LADJABLÈS

(Aside, laughing.)
I got news. We got the young man in the bag.
That's one of them in.
Now for the next!
(Turning to Eva.)
Well young lady,
as they say, let's get down to business.
You want to get to the other side, don't you?
But you must be prepared.
And you won't be prepared
if you can't dance to the beat.

EVA

We know how to dance.
We have our dances.

LADJABLÈS

We?
There's is only you and I here.
I don't know which we you're talking about!
Oh, I see. You're talking about the folk from Derrière Morne
and their movements to the noise of the drum.
Those that you said you brought from Africa.
Yes, the Soucouyant likes those
so I've learnt to tolerate them.
He is my connection to Derrière Morne, you know.
But my dear, you don't call these dances.
These have no place in decent spaces.
They're too…rough…if you know what I mean.
I will teach you the dances that you need, okay.
But before we get to the dance,
let us have a look at you.

LADJABLÈS (continued)

This body, I can see
longs for some exquisite attire.
That neck, those arms,
yearn for some fine jewellery, not so?
You want to be in the light,
all this you can have and more.
Come look, see down there, across the side of the hill.
See that gate there?
I hold the key and I can get you through there.
But you can't enter the light
like this. In this era,
you need a globalized image, you know.
So let's do something about your skin.
Take this. Rub some of it on your face.
Come on, be co-operative.
Rub it, I say! Ha! Ha! Ha! Ha!
Look at you!
Now you're fair!
An emerging power!
It's a brown thing, you know.
Yes, rub it along.
Now let us do something about your wool.
Again we have to globalize.
There's no excuse anymore for short hair!
Image, image, image! It's about tresses!
Down on your shoulders, falling on your back!
Now what is you're wearing! You call this a skirt?
No. This won't do! Not for strutting around Manhattan!
Put this on. And slip on these heels.
See? Now you're beginning to look the part!
Wait...you need just a little more boobs!
And some more bumps. We can fix that too!
Now let's see your hands! How ugly!
Have you been using a grater?
Your feet! Terrible!

LADJABLÈS (continued)

Cream! Cream! Cream!
Lots of white…or pink! Rub it in! Rub it in! Rub it in!
Here's some nail polish!
Polish! Polish! Polish!
Good!

EVA

(Aside.)
Why must I be forced into all this.
This hair, these nails,
this finery! It's all fake!

LADJABLÈS

(Overhearing.)
Image,
that's what counts.
And "fake" as you call it
is the only reality!
Ha! Ha! Ha! Ha! Ha!
Isn't this…ironic?
It's all one big show out there you know, honey!
No one wants reality…except if its Reality TV!
Ha! Ha! Ha! Ha! Another irony!
It's all about making the right impression.
Once you've done that, then you can retreat into whoever the hell you are,
but you've got to be fake to take.
You hear me?
You've got to be fake to take.
Repeat after me.
You've got to be fake to take
You've got to be fake to take
You've got to be fake to take.

(Eva repeats the line, the Ladjablés dances a jig around her seat with Eva following behind as she joins in the chant)

EVA AND LADJABLÈS

You've got to be fake to take
You've got to be fake to take
You've got to be fake to take.

EVA

(Exhausted, stops.)
Can I have the key, now?

LADJABLÈS

What?
Are you being stubborn?
The Key?

EVA

Yes, to the Secret Gate.

LADJABLÈS

(She laughs.)
That's the plot isn't it?
That you should climb the mountain
invade my territory,
make a mockery of me
while your boyfriend
remains in the village
and disrupts the work of the Soucouyant.
And then you both get the key,
the power to pass through my Secret Gate
and enter the land of opportunity.
and who knows you bring along the whole tribe of Derrière Morne!
Ha! Ha! Ha! Ha!
Well, let's see who is in control here!

(She snaps her fingers and a clarinet sounds. Ladjablès moves sensually, suggestively, The politicians, drug dealers, commercial representatives enter dressed in snake costumes perform a snake-like dance with her. The Ladjablès beckons Eva to do the same.)

LADJABLÈS

Now dance!

EVA

No, not here…more to this side.

LADJABLÈS

What? Right here!
You want the key or don't you?

EVA

Yes, but I…I ..I.
I must hear the drums.

LADJABLÈS

The drums?

EVA

Our drums.

LADJABLÈS

Ok, I'll oblige you.

EVA

(Eva dances to the drums)

LADJABLÈS

No!
Up the sound of the clarinet!
(Music plays: Jab-la kwiyé mwen.)

LADJABLÈS

Now move!

EVA

No. I won't.
Come into the circle,
into the Field.

LADJABLÈS

(She laughs)
You won't?
What field?

The Field of Power

EVA

The Field of Power.

LADJABLÈS

(She laughs)
Whose power?

EVA

Ours!

LADJABLÈS

There's no…ours!
You've been talking to my sister, haven't you?
Like her you want to learn the hard way? Okay then.
Dance, I say!
(She takes out a net and lunges at Eva, trapping her, and pulling her to her side. She shouts.)
Soucou! Send him out!

MAWON

(Emerging dazed.)
Eva, Eva…

(Sound of the clarinet. The Ladjablès stands astride Mawon who is lying on his back. She dances sensually.)

MADAME SAJÈS

(Enters. Speaks to Ladjablès.)
Leave the young man alone, you beast.

LADJABLÈS

What the hell, Sajès!
How dare you interfere?
Stay in your damn section!

MADAME SAJÈS

Eva! Your rosary!
Get out your rosary.
Say it Eva, pray with me.
The drums, where are the drums?

(Eva and Madanm Sajès pray to the rhythm of the drums.)

                    MADAME SAJÈS (continued)

Eva! Move toward the circle.
Up the sound of the drums.
We can defeat her.
It is time.
Mawon wake up!

LADJABLÈS

(Tries to sing but is overpowered and begins writhing in pain at the effect of the prayer.)
Soucou!
Soucou! My man!

(The Soucouyant appears at Ladjablès' side. Madame Sajès takes the net off Eva and, with Mawon's help, throws it over the Ladjablès and Soucouyant. Madame Sajès, Eva, and Mawon keep praying along with the sound of drum while they drag Ladjablès and Soucouyant into the circle. Mawon then pulls Eva into a long embrace. Eva then turns to gaze towards the Land of Opportunity. Kontè enters Stage Left leading the others and singing "Waya, Waya, Waya, Moulélé." Eva leads them slowly across the stage still gazing at the land of opportunity as they continue to sing. As they reach a crescendo with the song, lights fade to black.

They perform the curtain call to the song "*Si ou paka gouté'y, wo ou pa bon*" during which time Eva and Mawon free the Ladjablès and Soucouyant from the net.)

THE END

GLOSSARY

An mizi, an mizi: little by little.

Bazoudi: giddy, in a daze.

Bava: one who exaggerates, is talkative, boastful.

Bèlè Kont: a dance form, originally used as part of the narrative during the performance of the Kont.

Bétise: nonsense.

Cocomacaque: scheme, trick.

Débòt: a vigourous dance performed by a man and a woman facing each other, with continuous interplay of pelvic and leg movements.

Djiné: descendants of Guinea, West Africa who were brought to the Caribbean as indentured servants after emancipation.

Derrière Morne: literally-behind a hill, in "The Field of Power," the name of the village in which Eva and Mawon live.

Fanm: woman.

Fer-de-lance: a poisonous snake.

Fwidjé: banyan tree, also known as ficus.

Gadè: in this context a fortune teller but also a healer.

Gajé: one who practices magic (pejorative).

Gwajé: to grate.

Jumbies: walking dead or crack addicts on the streets.

Kèlè: a religious ceremony performed by descendants of the Djiné on the island of Saint Lucia in which a sheep is sacrificed to the gods ogun and shango.

Ki sa-an: what is it now?

Kouway: courage.

Kouyon: fool.

Kannòt: canoe, fishing boat

Konpè (fr.compere) comrade (affectionate) a title before the Christian name given to animal characters.

Kont: a narrative, a story told at wakes in memory of the deceased.

Kontè: storyteller.

Glossary

Ladjablès: (La Diablesse): evil woman in disguise. Usually white and beautiful with long flowing hair and a long dress that hides the cloven hoof that she instead of a foot.

L'histoire: story, history.

Manikou: an opossum.

Mépwis: dirty talk, usually delivered during a quarrel.

Negre Marron (Nèg Mawon): runaway slaves who set communities in the mountains.

Non: name.

Pòwyé: white cedar.

Sakwé: damn.

Sé: is

Secret band: a drumming group on the island of Saint Lucia.

Sikwiyé: a small yellow-breasted bird.

Solo: a musical form practised in Saint Lucia. A group of people move round and round in a circle to the sound of drums, chak-chak, and ti bwa (a percussion instrument made of a piece of bamboo laid horizontally and beaten with sticks).

Soucouyant: a figure from Caribbean folklore that sucks the blood out of humans.

Tanbou: drum played by descendants of Africans in the Caribbean.

Timanmay: child.

Towo: bull.

Vini: come.

www.ingramcontent.com/pod-product-compliance
Lightning Source LLC
Chambersburg PA
CBHW051804040426
42446CB00007B/504